The Beverage Book

Jean Paré

www.companyscoming.com
visit our ❦ website

Front Cover
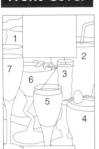

1. Melon Lemonade, page 124
2. Pineapple Mango Smoothie, page 10
3. Christmas Spirit, page 140
4. Purple Cow, page 57
5. Raspberry Spritzer, page 97
6. Orange Almond Cocktail, page 92
7. Cranberry Champagne, page 132

Props Courtesy Of:
Linens 'N Things
Stokes
Winners Stores

Back Cover

1. Almond Coffee, page 22
2. Sweet Dreams, page 103
3. Eggnog Cappuccino, page 28

Props Courtesy Of:
Canhome Global
Klass Works
Linens 'N Things
Stokes
The Bay
The Paderno Factory Store

We gratefully acknowledge the following suppliers for their generous support of our Test Kitchen and Photo Studio:

Broil King Barbecues
Corelle®
Hamilton Beach® Canada

Lagostina®
Proctor Silex® Canada
Tupperware®

The Beverage Book

Fourth Printing March 2006

National Library of Canada Cataloguing in Publication
Paré, Jean
The beverage book / Jean Paré.
(Original series)
Includes index.
ISBN 1-896891-88-8
1. Beverages. 2. Alcoholic beverages. I. Title. II. Series.
TX815.P37 2004   641.8'7   C2004-902500-7

Published by
Company's Coming Publishing Limited
2311 – 96 Street
Edmonton, Alberta, Canada T6N 1G3
Tel: 780-450-6223 Fax: 780-450-1857
www.companyscoming.com

Company's Coming is a registered trademark owned by Company's Coming Publishing Limited

Printed in Canada

Cooking tonight?

A selection of
feature recipes
is only a
click away—
absolutely ***FREE!***

Visit us at
www.companyscoming.com

Company's Coming Cookbooks

Original Series

- Softcover, 160 pages
- 6" x 9" (15 cm x 23 cm) format
- Lay-flat plastic comb binding
- Full-colour photos
- Nutrition information

Quick & easy recipes! Everyday ingredients!

Lifestyle Series

- Softcover, 160 pages
- 8" x 10" (20 cm x 25 cm) format
- Paperback
- Full-colour photos
- Nutrition information

Most Loved Recipe Collection

- Hardcover, 128 pages
- 8 3/4" x 8 3/4" (22 cm x 22 cm) format
- Durable sewn binding
- Full colour throughout
- Nutrition information

Special Occasion Series

- Hardcover & softcover, 192 pages
- 8 1/2" x 11" (22 cm x 28 cm) format
- Durable sewn binding
- Full colour throughout
- Nutrition information

See page 157 for more cookbooks.
For a complete listing, visit
www.companyscoming.com

Table of Contents

The Company's Coming Story

Jean Paré (pronounced "jeen PAIR-ee") grew up understanding that the combination of family, friends and home cooking is the best recipe for a good life. From her mother, she learned to appreciate good cooking, while her father praised even her earliest attempts in the kitchen. When Jean left home, she took with her a love of cooking, many family recipes and an intriguing desire to read cookbooks as if they were novels!

> *"never share a recipe you wouldn't use yourself"*

In 1963, when her four children had all reached school age, Jean volunteered to cater the 50th Anniversary of the Vermilion School of Agriculture, now Lakeland College, in Alberta, Canada. Working out of her home, Jean prepared a dinner for more than 1,000 people, which launched a flourishing catering operation that continued for over 18 years. During that time, she had countless opportunities to test new ideas with immediate feedback—resulting in empty plates and contented customers! Whether preparing cocktail sandwiches for a house party or serving a hot meal for 1,500 people, Jean Paré earned a reputation for good food, courteous service and reasonable prices.

As requests for her recipes mounted, Jean was often asked the question, "Why don't you write a cookbook?" Jean responded by teaming up with her son, Grant Lovig, in the fall of 1980 to form Company's Coming Publishing Limited. The publication of *150 Delicious Squares* on April 14, 1981 marked the debut of what would soon become one of the world's most popular cookbook series.

The company has grown since those early days when Jean worked from a spare bedroom in her home. Today, she continues to write recipes while working closely with the staff of the Recipe Factory, as the Company's Coming test kitchen is affectionately known. There she fills the role of mentor, assisting with the development of recipes people most want to use for everyday cooking and easy entertaining. Every Company's Coming recipe is *kitchen-tested* before it's approved for publication.

Jean's daughter, Gail Lovig, is responsible for marketing and distribution, leading a team that includes sales personnel located in major cities across Canada. In addition, Company's Coming cookbooks are published and

distributed under licence in the United States, Australia and other world markets. Bestsellers many times over in English, Company's Coming cookbooks have also been published in French and Spanish.

Familiar and trusted in home kitchens around the world, Company's Coming cookbooks are offered in a variety of formats. Highly regarded as kitchen workbooks, the softcover Original Series, with its lay-flat plastic comb binding, is still a favourite among readers.

Jean Paré's approach to cooking has always called for *quick and easy recipes* using *everyday ingredients.* That view has served her well. The recipient of many awards, including the Queen Elizabeth Golden Jubilee medal, Jean was appointed a Member of the Order of Canada, her country's highest lifetime achievement honour.

Jean continues to gain new supporters by adhering to what she calls The Golden Rule of Cooking: *"Never share a recipe you wouldn't use yourself."* It's an approach that works—*millions of times over!*

Foreword

We start and end our days with beverages, beginning with that first cup of steaming coffee or tea in the morning and ending with a soothing after-dinner drink or nightcap before bed. We celebrate memorable times with toasts and drink to good health! Beverages of all descriptions are an inseparable part of our daily lives. Finally, they are getting the attention they deserve.

Beverages have become much more than lunch or dinner accompaniments. They help create ambiance at elegant dinner parties or family get-togethers; they add comfort and warmth when you want to feel cozy; and they sparkle and bubble when you're laughing and celebrating.

In *The Beverage Book*, we've compiled more than 170 ways to quench your thirst, including long-time favourites you'll recognize, plus many special creations developed and tested in our own kitchen. Choose something hot or cold, sweet or savoury, with or without alcohol.

Get the energy and nutrition you need for breakfast with a satisfying smoothie or yummy shake. Spice up your coffee break with the taste of cinnamon, almond or vanilla, or try a sweet or tangy tea perfectly steeped. Add a fruity or extracted juice to your child's lunch, or make a vibrantly coloured, refreshing punch for your next birthday party or other special occasion. Put your feet up with a specialty coffee or a deliciously drowsy cocktail. Anything you could thirst for, we've provided—and more!

Hosting a party or family get-together? Try your hand at ice rings and fruit garnishes to add simple elegance, or serve your punch in a beautifully delicate or fantastically fun punch bowl. Need to know what glass is used with what drink? Check page 8 and

your presentation will always complement the delicious drink you've made. Wish you could make the perfect cup of coffee or tea? You can! We share our tips with you on page 9.

We've also added 24 ways to say, "Cheers!" in different languages, so you'll always have the right toast for that special moment with family and friends.

Whether you're preparing something steamy and sweet, or cool and quenching, *The Beverage Book* is a resource you won't want to be without.

Cheers!

Jean Paré

Each recipe has been analyzed using the most up-to-date version of the Canadian Nutrient File from Health Canada, which is based on the United States Department of Agriculture (USDA) Nutrient Data Base. If more than one ingredient is listed (such as "hard margarine or butter"), or a range is given (1 – 2 tsp., 5 – 10 mL), then the first ingredient or amount is used in the analysis. Where an ingredient reads "sprinkle," "optional," or "for garnish," it is not included as part of the nutrition information. Milk, unless stated otherwise, is 1% and cooking oil, unless stated otherwise, is canola.

Margaret Ng, B.Sc. (Hon), M.A.
Registered Dietitian

Serving Beverages

Alcoholic Beverages

When preparing cocktails with fruit juice, squeeze and strain the juice just before serving, then add the liquor. This keeps the taste of the juice vibrant and the taste of the alcohol strong. The suggested amount of alcohol per serving is 1 1/4 to 1 1/2 oz. (35 to 50 mL). For punches, keep all ingredients chilled, including the alcohol, until just before serving. This will keep the ice cubes or ice ring from melting too fast and keep the punch chilled longer.

Glasses

There are many different glass shapes and sizes to choose from when serving a beverage—and no glass is right or wrong. But in some cases there is a definite benefit to having a certain glass, as with a red wine glass where the deeper bowl shape captures the bouquet, or the fluted champagne glass that concentrates the effervescence at the top. We've identified five shapes that are reflected in the recipes in this book:

Champagne Flute: A tall, stemmed glass used for champagne and sparkling wine drinks. Holds 3/4 to 1 cup (175 to 250 mL).

Margarita Glass: A wide-rimmed, stemmed glass used for sipping slushy drinks. Rim is often dampened and dipped into salt or sugar. Holds 1 1/2 to 2 cups (375 to 500 mL).

Martini Glass: A wide-rimmed, stemmed glass with a triangular bowl used for martinis and other cocktails. Holds 1/2 to 3/4 cup (125 to 175 mL).

Red Wine and White Wine Glasses: The red wine glass has a slightly larger, deeper bowl. Holds 1 to 1 1/4 cups (250 to 300 mL). The white wine glass has a slightly smaller bowl. Holds 3/4 to 1 cup (175 to 250 mL).

The Perfect Cup Of...

Coffee

1. Use cold water (filtered water is best).

2. Use clean or well-rinsed equipment. If possible, wash your coffee maker after each use and store unassembled.

3. Buy small portions of coffee for immediate use or store unused coffee in a resealable container in the refrigerator. Do not mix old and new coffee.

4. Grind whole beans before brewing and always use the correct size of grind for your coffee maker.

5. Use 1 tbsp. (15 mL) ground coffee for each 8 oz. (1 cup, 250 mL) cold water for fairly weak strength, adding more to suit taste.

6. Serve coffee immediately after brewing and store in an insulated carafe for up to an hour. Do not keep coffee on stove element or base of coffee machine. Do not boil or it will become bitter; do not reheat because it will taste stale.

Tea

1. Heat water (filtered is best) to just boiling.

2. Rinse teapot with hot water to minimize cooling of hot water when added.

3. Use 1 tea bag (or 1 tbsp., 15 mL, loose tea) for each cup.

4. Steep tea for 3 to 6 minutes, depending on type (green tea should steep for 2 to 3 minutes; black for 4 to 5 minutes).

5. Remove tea bag or strain loose tea.

6. For a stronger tea, add more tea bags rather than steeping tea longer than the recommended time. Steeping for too long causes bitterness. For a weaker tea, add more hot water.

7. Loose tea is best for flavour because the leaves can expand. Tea bags restrict the expansion of the leaves necessary for achieving full flavour.

8. Store tea in an airtight, opaque container in a cool, dry place or in tightly closing metal tins. Clear glass jars are acceptable if kept in a closed cupboard away from light. Do not refrigerate.

Glass & Mug sizes used in this book:

Small glass	4 to 8 oz.	125 to 250 mL
Medium glass	8 to 12 oz.	250 to 375 mL
Large glass	12 to 16 oz.	375 to 500 mL
Small mug	6 to 8 oz.	175 to 250 mL
Large mug	8 to 12 oz.	250 to 375 mL

Cantaloupe Smoothie

Have you ever had a melon smoothie? Here's a great one to try,
with just a hint of cinnamon!

Ripe medium banana, cut up	1	1
Cantaloupe, seeds removed, chopped	1/2	1/2
Plain yogurt	1 1/2 cups	375 mL
Liquid honey	2 tbsp.	30 mL
Ground cinnamon	1/4 tsp.	1 mL
Ice cubes	6	6

Process all 6 ingredients in blender until smooth. Makes about 4 1/2 cups
(1.1 L). Pour into 4 medium glasses. Serves 4.

1 serving: 144 Calories; 1.8 g Total Fat (0.4 g Mono, 0.1 g Poly, 1 g Sat); 6 mg Cholesterol;
28 g Carbohydrate; 1 g Fibre; 6 g Protein; 75 mg Sodium

Pineapple Mango Smoothie

Flavour of the tropics. Thick and refreshing.

Chopped fresh pineapple (or can of pineapple tidbits, 8 oz., 227 mL, drained)	1 cup	250 mL
Ripe medium mango, diced	1	1
Orange juice	1 cup	250 mL
Ice cubes	6	6
Coconut flavouring	1/16 tsp.	0.5 mL

Process all 5 ingredients in blender until smooth. Makes about 3 1/3 cups
(825 mL). Pour into 2 large glasses. Serves 2.

1 serving: 166 Calories; 0.9 g Total Fat (0.2 g Mono, 0.2 g Poly, 0.1 g Sat); 0 mg Cholesterol;
41 g Carbohydrate; 3 g Fibre; 2 g Protein; 4 mg Sodium

Pictured on front cover.

Raspberry Energizer

Thick, pink drink bursting with raspberry flavour.

Frozen whole raspberries	1 cup	250 mL
Raspberry yogurt	1 cup	250 mL
Soy milk (or milk)	1 cup	250 mL
Raspberry jam	2 tbsp.	30 mL
Large egg (see Note)	1	1

Process all 5 ingredients in blender until smooth. Makes about 3 cups (750 mL). Pour into 2 large glasses. Serves 2.

1 serving: 291 Calories; 7.3 g Total Fat (2 g Mono, 1.7 g Poly, 2.3 g Sat); 116 mg Cholesterol; 46 g Carbohydrate; 4 g Fibre; 12 g Protein; 119 mg Sodium

Pictured on page 17.

Note: Eggs used in beverages should be cold. Remove egg from refrigerator just before adding. Beverages containing uncooked egg should be served immediately.

Yogurt Fruit Smoothie

Very sweet, very pretty beverage with a whisper of cinnamon.

Fresh strawberries	8	8
Ripe medium banana, cut up	1	1
Vanilla yogurt	1 1/2 cups	375 mL
Frozen blueberries	1/2 cup	125 mL
Frozen concentrated orange juice	2 tbsp.	30 mL
Ground cinnamon	1/8 tsp.	0.5 mL
Ice cubes	3	3

Process all 7 ingredients in blender until smooth. Makes about 3 3/4 cups (925 mL). Pour into 4 small glasses. Serves 4.

1 serving: 149 Calories; 2.3 g Total Fat (0.5 g Mono, 0.1 g Poly, 1.3 g Sat); 5 mg Cholesterol; 30 g Carbohydrate; 2 g Fibre; 5 g Protein; 57 mg Sodium

Energy Burst

Tart cranberry, creamy strawberry and nutty wheat germ.
Tastes good—and is good for you!

Cranberry cocktail	2 cups	500 mL
Fresh (or frozen whole) strawberries, chopped	1 cup	250 mL
Strawberry frozen yogurt	1/2 cup	125 mL
Wheat germ, toasted (see Tip, page 13)	2 tbsp.	30 mL

Process all 4 ingredients in blender until smooth. Makes about 3 cups (750 mL). Pour into 2 large glasses. Serves 2.

1 serving: 286 Calories; 4.1 g Total Fat (0.9 g Mono, 0.7 g Poly, 2 g Sat); 5 mg Cholesterol; 61 g Carbohydrate; 3 g Fibre; 4 g Protein; 38 mg Sodium

PB And Banana Toast

The taste of a peanut butter and banana sandwich—in a glass!
For the kid in all of us!

Frozen ripe medium bananas (see Tip, page 21)	2	2
Milk	2 cups	500 mL
Smooth peanut butter	1/4 cup	60 mL
Wheat germ, toasted (see Tip, page 13)	3 tbsp.	50 mL
Liquid honey	2 tbsp.	30 mL
Vanilla	1/8 tsp.	0.5 mL

Process all 6 ingredients in blender until smooth. Makes about 4 cups (1 L). Pour into 4 medium glasses. Serves 4.

1 serving: 269 Calories; 10.9 g Total Fat (4.7 g Mono, 2.8 g Poly, 2.8 g Sat); 5 mg Cholesterol; 35 g Carbohydrate; 3 g Fibre; 10 g Protein; 147 mg Sodium

Kiwi Yogurt Smoothie

Creamy, tangy smoothie with a touch of sweetness.

Ripe kiwifruit, peeled and chopped	2	2
Vanilla frozen yogurt	1 cup	250 mL
Orange juice	1 cup	250 mL
Liquid honey	1 tbsp.	15 mL

Process all 4 ingredients in blender until smooth. Makes about 2 1/4 cups (550 mL). Pour into 2 medium glasses. Serves 2.

1 serving: 259 Calories; 4.9 g Total Fat (1.3 g Mono, 0.2 g Poly, 2.6 g Sat); 2 mg Cholesterol; 52 g Carbohydrate; 3 g Fibre; 5 g Protein; 72 mg Sodium

Pictured on page 17.

Sunshine Cup

A bright-coloured, fruit-flavoured breakfast delight.
Good morning, sunshine!

Apricot nectar	4 cups	1 L
Can of pineapple tidbits (with juice)	14 oz.	398 mL
Frozen concentrated orange juice	1/4 cup	60 mL

Measure 2 cups (500 mL) apricot nectar, 1/2 can of pineapple tidbits and 2 tbsp. (30 mL) frozen concentrated orange juice into blender. Process until smooth. Transfer to large pitcher. Repeat with remaining apricot nectar, pineapple and concentrated orange juice. Makes about 7 cups (1.75 L). Pour into 6 medium glasses. Serves 6.

1 serving: 161 Calories; 0.2 g Total Fat (0.1 g Mono, 0.1 g Poly, 0 g Sat); 0 mg Cholesterol; 41 g Carbohydrate; 2 g Fibre; 1 g Protein; 6 mg Sodium

 To toast wheat germ, spread evenly in ungreased shallow pan. Bake in 350°F (175°C) oven for about 3 minutes, stirring or shaking often until golden, or heat and stir in small frying pan on medium. Let stand until cooled completely.

Apricot Pick-Me-Up

Buttermilk with apricot and pineapple in a light, foamy drink.
A great way to start your day! Store leftover apricot halves in light syrup
in an airtight container in the fridge and use in other beverages.

Apricot nectar	1/2 cup	125 mL
Pineapple juice	1/2 cup	125 mL
Buttermilk	1/3 cup	75 mL
Canned apricot halves (about 4 halves)	1/4 cup	60 mL
Milk	1/4 cup	60 mL

Process all 5 ingredients in blender until smooth and frothy. Makes about 2 cups (500 mL). Pour into 2 medium glasses. Serve immediately. Serves 2.

1 serving: 120 Calories; 0.9 g Total Fat (0.3 g Mono, 0.1 g Poly, 0.5 g Sat); 3 mg Cholesterol; 26 g Carbohydrate; 1 g Fibre; 3 g Protein; 66 mg Sodium

Razzmatazz

Apricot nectar adds an unexpected, delightful flavour
to this thick raspberry smoothie.

Frozen whole raspberries	1 cup	250 mL
Apricot nectar	1 cup	250 mL
Vanilla yogurt	1/2 cup	125 mL
Liquid honey	2 tbsp.	30 mL
Ice cubes	6	6

Process all 5 ingredients in blender until smooth. Makes about 2 3/4 cups (675 mL). Pour into 2 medium glasses. Serves 2.

1 serving: 230 Calories; 1.7 g Total Fat (0.4 g Mono, 0.3 g Poly, 0.8 g Sat); 3 mg Cholesterol; 54 g Carbohydrate; 4 g Fibre; 4 g Protein; 42 mg Sodium

Banana Shake

Banana and maple make a pleasantly sweet and creamy shake.

Ripe medium banana, cut up	1	1
Milk	1 1/2 cups	375 mL
Vanilla ice cream	1 cup	250 mL
Maple (or maple-flavoured) syrup	2 tbsp.	30 mL

Process all 4 ingredients in blender until smooth. Makes about 2 3/4 cups (675 mL). Pour into 2 medium glasses. Serves 2.

1 serving: 326 Calories; 10 g Total Fat (2.8 g Mono, 0.4 g Poly, 6.1 g Sat); 38 mg Cholesterol; 53 g Carbohydrate; 1 g Fibre; 9 g Protein; 155 mg Sodium

Soy Delicious

Enjoyable because it's sweet, thick and frothy.

Frozen ripe medium banana (see Tip, page 21)	1	1
Soy milk (or milk)	1 1/2 cups	375 mL
Vanilla yogurt	1/2 cup	125 mL
Wheat germ	2 tbsp.	30 mL
Maple (or maple-flavoured) syrup	1 tbsp.	15 mL

Process all 5 ingredients in blender until smooth. Makes about 3 cups (750 mL). Pour into 4 small glasses. Serves 4.

1 serving: 114 Calories; 2.9 g Total Fat (0.5 g Mono, 1.1 g Poly, 0.7 g Sat); 2 mg Cholesterol; 19 g Carbohydrate; 2 g Fibre; 5 g Protein; 31 mg Sodium

Paré Pointer
Say cheers in Austrian: "Prosit!" (PROH-sit)

Citrus Shake

Silky papaya with the tang of grapefruit and orange.
Great citrus combo.

Ruby red grapefruit juice	1 cup	250 mL
Chopped papaya	1 cup	250 mL
Vanilla frozen yogurt	1 cup	250 mL
Frozen concentrated orange juice	2 tbsp.	30 mL

Process all 4 ingredients in blender until smooth. Makes about 2 1/2 cups (625 mL). Pour into 2 medium glasses. Serves 2.

1 serving: 239 Calories; 4.5 g Total Fat (1.3 g Mono, 0.2 g Poly, 2.7 g Sat); 2 mg Cholesterol; 47 g Carbohydrate; 2 g Fibre; 5 g Protein; 72 mg Sodium

Pictured on page 17.

1. Kiwi Yogurt Smoothie, page 13
2. Raspberry Energizer, page 11
3. Citrus Shake, above

Props Courtesy Of: Danesco Inc.

Breakfast Drinks

Apple-A-Day

A quick, tasty way to get your "apple a day." Tart and creamy.
Add more honey if you like a sweeter taste.

Apple juice	2 cups	500 mL
Unsweetened applesauce	1 cup	250 mL
Plain (or soy) yogurt	1/2 cup	125 mL
Frozen concentrated apple juice	2 tbsp.	30 mL
Liquid honey	1 tbsp.	15 mL

Ground cinnamon, sprinkle (optional)

Process first 5 ingredients in blender until smooth and frothy. Makes about 3 1/2 cups (875 mL). Pour into 2 large glasses.

Sprinkle each with cinnamon. Serves 2.

1 serving: 281 Calories; 1.4 g Total Fat (0.3 g Mono, 0.2 g Poly, 0.7 g Sat); 4 mg Cholesterol; 66 g Carbohydrate; 2 g Fibre; 4 g Protein; 61 mg Sodium

1. Almond Coffee, page 22
2. Sweet Dreams, page 103
3. Eggnog Cappuccino, page 28

Props Courtesy Of: Canhome Global
Klass Works
Linens 'N Things
Stokes
The Bay
The Paderno Factory Store

Orchard Shake Up

Loads of natural sweetness in this creamy shake.

Can of pear halves (with juice)	14 oz.	398 mL
Chopped pitted dates	1/2 cup	125 mL
Frozen concentrated apple juice	2 tbsp.	30 mL
Vanilla frozen yogurt	1 cup	250 mL
Milk	1 cup	250 mL

Process first 3 ingredients in blender until fruit is finely chopped.

Add frozen yogurt and milk. Process until smooth. Makes about 4 cups (1 L). Pour into 4 medium glasses. Serves 4.

1 serving: 219 Calories; 3 g Total Fat (0.8 g Mono, 0.1 g Poly, 1.7 g Sat); 3 mg Cholesterol; 47 g Carbohydrate; 4 g Fibre; 5 g Protein; 72 mg Sodium

Very Berry Frappé

Very berry cold and refreshing. A zesty drink to wake up to.

Frozen mixed berries	2 cups	500 mL
Milk (or soy milk)	1 cup	250 mL
Dessert tofu (such as Pete's Tofu Very Berry-flavoured dessert), or plain soft tofu	3/4 cup	175 mL
Cranberry cocktail	1/2 cup	125 mL
Liquid honey	1 tbsp.	15 mL

Process all 5 ingredients in blender until smooth. Makes about 3 1/4 cups (800 mL). Pour into 2 large glasses. Serves 2.

1 serving: 277 Calories; 6.5 g Total Fat (1.4 g Mono, 2.7 g Poly, 1.5 g Sat); 5 mg Cholesterol; 47 g Carbohydrate; 7 g Fibre; 13 g Protein; 75 mg Sodium

Wake-Up Call

Peach and honey with the subtle taste of soy.
A light beverage with just a bit of tang.

Can of sliced peaches in light syrup (with juice)	14 oz.	398 mL
Soy milk (or milk)	1 cup	250 mL
Lite silken firm tofu, chopped	3/4 cup	175 mL
Liquid honey	2 tbsp.	30 mL
Vanilla	1/2 tsp.	2 mL

Process all 5 ingredients in blender until smooth. Makes about 3 cups (750 mL). Pour into 2 large glasses. Serves 2.

1 serving: 342 Calories; 11.4 g Total Fat (2.4 g Mono, 6.1 g Poly, 1.6 g Sat); 0 mg Cholesterol; 47 g Carbohydrate; 2 g Fibre; 20 g Protein; 41 mg Sodium

 To use overripe bananas, peel and cut them into 2 inch (5 cm) pieces. Arrange in single layer in ungreased 9 x 13 inch (22 x 33 cm) pan. Freeze until firm. Store in resealable freezer bag. Substitute 4 pieces for 1 medium banana. Overripe bananas provide rich flavour to beverages.

Almond Coffee

A rich, dark, fragrant coffee. Perfect for after dinner.

Hot strong prepared coffee (see Note)	2 cups	500 mL
Almond-flavoured liqueur (such as Amaretto), 2 oz.	1/4 cup	60 mL
Half-and-half cream (or milk)	2 tbsp.	30 mL
Brown sugar, packed	2 tsp.	10 mL
Whipped cream (or frozen whipped topping, thawed)	1/4 cup	60 mL
Sliced almonds, toasted (see Tip, page 23)	1 tbsp.	15 mL
Cocoa, sifted if lumpy (sprinkle)		

Combine first 4 ingredients in 4 cup (1 L) liquid measure or small heatproof pitcher. Makes about 2 1/4 cups (550 mL). Pour into 2 large mugs.

Top each with whipped cream. Sprinkle almonds and cocoa over top. Serves 2.

1 serving: 246 Calories; 8.5 g Total Fat (3.1 g Mono, 0.6 g Poly, 4.3 g Sat); 23 mg Cholesterol; 23 g Carbohydrate; trace Fibre; 2 g Protein; 26 mg Sodium

Pictured on page 18 and on back cover.

Note: For extra-strong flavour, use espresso.

Variation (without alcohol): Omit liqueur. Use same amount of almond-flavoured syrup (such as Torani's).

Paré Pointer

Say cheers in Japanese: "Kampai!" (KAM-pay)

Spiced Iced Coffee

Sweet, smooth, dark coffee—cool and refreshing.

Hot strong prepared coffee (see Note)	4 cups	1 L
Granulated sugar	1/3 cup	75 mL
Cinnamon sticks (4 inches, 10 cm, each)	4	4
Whole cloves	6	6
Coffee-flavoured liqueur (such as Kahlúa), 2 oz.	1/4 cup	60 mL
Ice		

Measure first 4 ingredients into medium bowl. Stir until sugar is dissolved. Chill for 1 1/2 to 2 hours until cold.

Strain coffee mixture through sieve into pitcher. Discard solids. Add liqueur. Stir. Makes about 4 cups (1 L).

Pour over ice in 4 medium glasses. Serves 4.

1 serving: 140 Calories; 0.1 g Total Fat (0 g Mono, 0 g Poly, 0 g Sat); 0 mg Cholesterol; 28 g Carbohydrate; 0 g Fibre; 1 g Protein; 12 mg Sodium

Note: For extra-strong flavour, use espresso.

Variation (without alcohol): Omit liqueur. Use same amount of coffee-flavoured syrup (such as Torani's).

Serving Suggestion: Garnish with fresh cinnamon sticks.

 To toast seeds, nuts and coconut, spread evenly in ungreased shallow pan. Bake in 350ºF (175ºC) oven for 5 to 10 minutes, stirring or shaking often, until desired doneness.

Café Olé

Coffee with a sweet, Mexican twist.

ORANGE DREAM TOPPING

Whipping cream	1/2 cup	125 mL
Orange Dream Liqueur, page 139 (or brandy), 2 oz.	1/4 cup	60 mL
Icing (confectioner's) sugar	1 tbsp.	15 mL
Hot strong prepared coffee (see Note)	4 cups	1 L
Whipping cream	1/2 cup	125 mL
Coffee-flavoured liqueur (such as Kahlúa), 2 oz.	1/4 cup	60 mL
Cocoa, sifted if lumpy	2 tbsp.	30 mL
Ground cinnamon	1/2 tsp.	2 mL

Orange Dream Topping: Beat first 3 ingredients in small bowl until soft peaks form. Makes about 1 cup (250 mL) topping. Chill.

Measure next 5 ingredients into heatproof pitcher. Stir well. Makes about 5 cups (1.25 L). Pour into 4 large mugs. Spoon 1/4 cup (60 mL) topping onto each. Serves 4.

1 serving: 319 Calories; 21.2 g Total Fat (6.2 g Mono, 0.7 g Poly, 13.2 g Sat); 75 mg Cholesterol; 22 g Carbohydrate; 1 g Fibre; 3 g Protein; 43 mg Sodium

Note: For extra-strong flavour, use espresso.

Serving Suggestion: Sprinkle finely grated orange zest over topping for added zip!

Paré Pointer
Say cheers in Finnish: "Kippis!" (KIP-his)

Coffee Drinks

Café Vienna

This delicious brew will warm you up on a chilly evening.

Milk	1 cup	250 mL
Instant coffee granules	1 1/2 tsp.	7 mL
Ground cinnamon, just a pinch		
Chocolate-flavoured liqueur (such as Crème de cacao), 1 oz.	2 tbsp.	30 mL

Heat and stir milk, coffee granules and cinnamon in small heavy saucepan on medium until bubbles form around edge. Remove from heat.

Add liqueur. Stir. Makes about 1 cup (250 mL). Pour into small mug. Serves 1.

1 serving: 216 Calories; 7.7 g Total Fat (2.2 g Mono, 0.3 g Poly, 4.8 g Sat); 15 mg Cholesterol; 20 g Carbohydrate; 0 g Fibre; 10 g Protein; 159 mg Sodium

Serving Suggestion: For added flair, dip rim of mug into liqueur in saucer. Press rim into granulated sugar in separate saucer until coated.

Canadian Coffee

Appealing maple flavour. Not just for pancakes anymore!

Hot prepared coffee	3/4 cup	175 mL
Maple-flavoured liqueur (such as Wild Maple Cream), 1/2 oz.	1 tbsp.	15 mL
Canadian whisky (rye), 1/2 oz.	1 tbsp.	15 mL
Whipped cream (or frozen whipped topping, thawed)	2 tbsp.	30 mL

Measure hot coffee, liqueur and whisky into small mug. Stir. Makes about 1 cup (250 mL).

Top with whipped cream. Serves 1.

1 serving: 134 Calories; 7.3 g Total Fat (2.1 g Mono, 0.3 g Poly, 4.6 g Sat); 20 mg Cholesterol; 5 g Carbohydrate; 0 g Fibre; 1 g Protein; 24 mg Sodium

Cinnamon Iced Coffee

Distinct cinnamon flavour in a cold coffee float. A summer's day drink.

Hot strong prepared coffee (see Note)	2 cups	500 mL
Granulated sugar	3 tbsp.	50 mL
Milk	3 cups	750 mL
Cinnamon sticks (4 inches, 10 cm, each)	3	3
Vanilla ice cream	2 cups	500 mL
White sanding (decorating) sugar, for garnish (see Note)	2 tsp.	10 mL
Ground cinnamon, for garnish	1/8 tsp.	0.5 mL

Measure hot coffee and granulated sugar into heatproof pitcher. Stir until sugar is dissolved. Let stand for 5 minutes.

Add milk to coffee mixture. Stir. Add cinnamon sticks. Cover. Chill for at least 4 hours until cold. Remove and discard cinnamon sticks. Makes about 5 cups (1.25 L) iced coffee.

Put 1/2 cup (125 mL) ice cream (about 2 scoops) into each of 4 chilled large glasses. Divide and pour coffee mixture over ice cream.

Combine sanding sugar and cinnamon in small cup. Sprinkle over each. Serves 4.

1 serving: 263 Calories; 9.7 g Total Fat (2.8 g Mono, 0.4 g Poly, 6 g Sat); 38 mg Cholesterol; 36 g Carbohydrate; 0 g Fibre; 9 g Protein; 158 mg Sodium

Pictured on page 35.

Note: For extra-strong flavour, use espresso.

Note: Sanding sugar is a coarse decorating sugar that comes in white and various colours and is available at specialty kitchen stores.

Licorice Cream Coffee

Creamy coffee with a touch of licorice. Mmm....

Hot prepared coffee	3/4 cup	175 mL
Irish cream liqueur (such as Baileys), 1 oz.	2 tbsp.	30 mL
Licorice-flavoured liqueur (such as Sambuca), 1/4 oz.	1/2 tbsp.	7 mL
Whipped cream (or frozen whipped topping, thawed), optional	2 tbsp.	30 mL

Measure hot coffee and both liqueurs into small mug. Stir. Makes about 1 cup (250 mL).

Top with whipped cream. Serves 1.

1 serving: 139 Calories; 5 g Total Fat (1.4 g Mono, 0.2 g Poly, 3.1 g Sat); 5 mg Cholesterol; 11 g Carbohydrate; 0 g Fibre; 1 g Protein; 33 mg Sodium

Maple Iced Coffee

Thick and creamy, maple-flavoured dessert coffee. Serve with a spoon or straw.

Cold strong prepared coffee (see Note)	1 1/2 cups	375 mL
Maple (or vanilla) ice cream, softened	1 cup	250 mL
Maple (or maple-flavoured) syrup	2 tbsp.	30 mL
Ice cubes	6	6

Process all 4 ingredients in blender until smooth. Makes about 2 cups (500 mL). Pour into 2 chilled medium glasses. Serves 2.

1 serving: 200 Calories; 7.7 g Total Fat (2.2 g Mono, 0.3 g Poly, 4.7 g Sat); 31 mg Cholesterol; 31 g Carbohydrate; 0 g Fibre; 3 g Protein; 65 mg Sodium

Pictured on page 35.

Note: For extra-strong flavour, use espresso.

Coffee Granita

Strong, icy and sweet with a cinnamon kick. Exhilarating!

Hot strong prepared coffee (see Note)	2 cups	500 mL
Brown sugar, packed	3 tbsp.	50 mL
Ground cinnamon	1/4 tsp.	1 mL
Coffee-flavoured liqueur (such as Kahlúa), 2 oz.	1/4 cup	60 mL

Measure hot coffee, brown sugar and cinnamon into medium bowl. Stir until sugar is dissolved. Pour into 1 quart (1 L) shallow baking dish. Cover. Freeze for about 3 hours until almost firm. Makes about 2 cups (500 mL) slush.

Scrape coffee mixture, using fork, into 2 chilled medium glasses. Drizzle 2 tbsp. (30 mL) liqueur over each. Serves 2.

1 serving: 214 Calories; 0.1 g Total Fat (0 g Mono, 0 g Poly, 0 g Sat); 0 mg Cholesterol; 40 g Carbohydrate; 0 g Fibre; 1 g Protein; 21 mg Sodium

Pictured on page 35.

Note: For extra-strong flavour, use espresso.

Serving Suggestion: Serve this coffee in a martini glass (see page 8) for a classy touch.

Eggnog Cappuccino

Deliciously strong coffee with creamy eggnog and cinnamon.
Impressive presentation—festive and flavourful!

Hot strong prepared coffee (see Note)	1/2 cup	125 mL
Eggnog, warmed	2/3 cup	150 mL
Ground cinnamon, sprinkle (optional)		

Pour hot coffee into 2 small mugs.

Beat eggnog with whisk until frothy, or use milk frother. Spoon over top of coffee. Sprinkle each with cinnamon. Serves 2.

1 serving: 123 Calories; 6.7 g Total Fat (2 g Mono, 0.3 g Poly, 4 g Sat); 53 mg Cholesterol; 13 g Carbohydrate; 0 g Fibre; 4 g Protein; 51 mg Sodium

Pictured on page 18 and on back cover.

Note: For extra-strong flavour, use espresso.

Spiced Honey Coffee

Honey and spice make coffee so nice!

Milk	1/2 cup	125 mL
Liquid honey	2 tbsp.	30 mL
Vanilla	1/4 tsp.	1 mL
Ground cinnamon	1/8 tsp.	0.5 mL
Ground nutmeg, just a pinch		
Hot strong prepared coffee (see Note)	1 1/4 cups	300 mL
Whipped cream (or frozen whipped topping, thawed), for garnish	1/3 cup	75 mL

Heat and stir first 5 ingredients in small heavy saucepan on medium for about 5 minutes until bubbles form around edge and milk just starts to boil.

Pour milk mixture into 2 small mugs. Add hot coffee to each. Makes about 2 cups (500 mL).

Top each with whipped cream. Serves 2.

1 serving: 100 Calories; 0.7 g Total Fat (0.2 g Mono, 0 g Poly, 0.4 g Sat); 3 mg Cholesterol; 22 g Carbohydrate; 0 g Fibre; 3 g Protein; 39 mg Sodium

Note: For extra-strong flavour, use espresso.

Serving Suggestion: Add a cinnamon stick—makes a pretty garnish and a great stir stick as well!

Paré Pointer
Say cheers in Chinese: "Ganbei!" (GAHN-bay)

Orange Liqueur Coffee

Barely sweet, dark coffee with creamy orange topping.

ORANGE CREAM TOPPING

Whipping cream	1/2 cup	125 mL
Orange-flavoured liqueur (such as Grand Marnier), 1/2 oz.	1 tbsp.	15 mL
Granulated sugar	1 tbsp.	15 mL
Hot strong prepared coffee (see Note)	3 cups	750 mL
Orange-flavoured liqueur (such as Grand Marnier), 1 oz.	2 tbsp.	30 mL
Coffee-flavoured liqueur (such as Kahlúa), 1 oz.	2 tbsp.	30 mL

Cocoa, sifted if lumpy (sprinkle)

Orange Cream Topping: Beat whipping cream, first amount of liqueur and sugar in small bowl until soft peaks form. Makes about 1 cup (250 mL) topping.

Combine next 3 ingredients in 4 cup (1 L) liquid measure or small heatproof pitcher. Makes about 3 cups (750 mL). Pour into 4 small mugs. Spoon 1/4 cup (60 mL) topping onto each.

Sprinkle each with cocoa. Serves 4.

1 serving: 169 Calories; 10.1 g Total Fat (3 g Mono, 0.3 g Poly, 6.3 g Sat); 37 mg Cholesterol; 10 g Carbohydrate; 0 g Fibre; 1 g Protein; 20 mg Sodium

Note: For extra-strong flavour, use espresso.

Irish Coffee

Toast the Irish with this traditional drink.

Irish whiskey (1 1/2 oz.)	3 tbsp.	50 mL
Granulated sugar	1/2 tsp.	2 mL
Hot strong prepared coffee (see Note)	3/4 cup	175 mL
Whipped cream (or frozen whipped topping, thawed)	2 tbsp.	30 mL

Measure whiskey and sugar into small mug. Add hot coffee. Stir. Makes about 1 cup (250 mL).

Top with whipped cream. Serves 1.

1 serving: 159 Calories; 4.9 g Total Fat (1.4 g Mono, 0.2 g Poly, 3 g Sat); 18 mg Cholesterol; 4 g Carbohydrate; 0 g Fibre; 1 g Protein; 13 mg Sodium

Note: For extra-strong flavour, use espresso.

Irish Cream Floats

Ice cream and liqueur make this coffee a rich, creamy dessert to eat with a spoon!

Hot strong prepared coffee (see Note)	1 1/2 cups	375 mL
Brown sugar, packed	1 tbsp.	15 mL
Irish cream liqueur (such as Baileys), 2 1/2 oz.	1/3 cup	75 mL
Chocolate ice cream	1 cup	250 mL

Measure hot coffee and brown sugar into 2 cup (500 mL) liquid measure. Stir until sugar is dissolved. Add liqueur. Stir. Makes about 2 cups (500 mL). Pour into 2 chilled large glasses or mugs.

Add 1/2 cup (125 mL) ice cream (about 2 scoops) to each. Serves 2.

1 serving: 353 Calories; 14.5 g Total Fat (4.2 g Mono, 0.6 g Poly, 9 g Sat); 30 mg Cholesterol; 44 g Carbohydrate; 0 g Fibre; 4 g Protein; 106 mg Sodium

Note: For extra-strong flavour, use espresso.

Variation (without alcohol): Omit liqueur. Use same amount of Irish cream-flavoured syrup (such as Torani's).

Caramel Chocolate

Dessert in a mug! Sweet, smooth, caramel-flavoured coffee.
Caramelizing the milk takes time, but it's definitely worth it.

Can of sweetened condensed milk	11 oz.	300 mL
Hot strong prepared coffee (see Note)	4 cups	1 L
Chocolate syrup	1/4 cup	60 mL

Pour condensed milk into 9 inch (22 cm) glass pie plate. Cover tightly with foil. Placed in medium roasting pan. Pour hot water into roasting pan until 1 inch (2.5 cm) deep. Bake in 425°F (220°C) oven for about 80 minutes until milk is thickened and caramel-coloured. Remove pie plate from roasting pan. Transfer caramelized milk to large bowl.

Add hot coffee and chocolate syrup. Stir well. Makes about 5 cups (1.25 L). Spoon into 6 small mugs. Serves 6.

1 serving: 243 Calories; 5.8 g Total Fat (1.6 g Mono, 0.2 g Poly, 3.6 g Sat); 22 mg Cholesterol; 44 g Carbohydrate; 0 g Fibre; 6 g Protein; 102 mg Sodium

Note: For extra-strong flavour, use espresso.

To Make Ahead: Prepare caramelized milk. Cover. Chill until ready to use. Place caramelized milk in medium saucepan. Add hot coffee and chocolate syrup. Heat on medium-low, stirring occasionally, until hot. Do not boil. Serve immediately.

Cocoa-Nut Coffee

You'll enjoy the hazelnut aroma of this coffee topped
with a rich chocolate cream. So tempting.

COCOA CREAM TOPPING

Whipping cream	1/2 cup	125 mL
Granulated sugar	1 tbsp.	15 mL
Cocoa, sifted if lumpy	1 tsp.	5 mL
Hot prepared coffee	4 cups	1 L
Hazelnut-flavoured liqueur (such as Frangelico), 4 oz.	1/2 cup	125 mL

(continued on next page)

Cocoa Cream Topping: Beat whipping cream, sugar and cocoa in small bowl until stiff peaks form. Makes about 1 cup (250 mL) topping.

Pour hot coffee into 4 large mugs. Add 2 tbsp. (30 mL) liqueur to each. Stir. Spoon 1/4 cup (60 mL) topping onto each. Serves 4.

1 serving: 226 Calories; 10.3 g Total Fat (3 g Mono, 0.4 g Poly, 6.4 g Sat); 37 mg Cholesterol; 17 g Carbohydrate; trace Fibre; 1 g Protein; 19 mg Sodium

Variation (without alcohol): Omit liqueur. Use same amount of hazelnut-flavoured syrup (such as Torani's).

Serving Suggestion: Garnish with chocolate curls or sprinkle with cocoa for added appeal and taste.

Chocolate Coffee

Chocolate in creamy, hot coffee. A luscious treat.
Use homogenized milk for a richer flavour.

Milk	1 cup	250 mL
Chopped dark chocolate (about 1 3/4 oz., 50 g)	1/4 cup	60 mL
Granulated sugar	3 tbsp.	50 mL
Milk	4 cups	1 L
Hot strong prepared coffee (see Note)	3 cups	750 mL
Vanilla	1 tsp.	5 mL
Large marshmallows	12	12

Heat and stir first 3 ingredients in large heavy saucepan on medium-low for 8 to 10 minutes until chocolate is melted.

Slowly add second amount of milk, stirring constantly. Increase heat to medium. Heat and stir until mixture is hot.

Add hot coffee and vanilla. Stir well. Makes about 8 cups (2 L). Pour into 6 large mugs.

Top each with 2 marshmallows. Serves 6.

1 serving: 203 Calories; 4.5 g Total Fat (1.4 g Mono, 0.2 g Poly, 2.7 g Sat); 9 mg Cholesterol; 34 g Carbohydrate; trace Fibre; 8 g Protein; 120 mg Sodium

Note: For extra-strong flavour, use espresso.

Apple Iced Tea

Fruity amber tea sweetened with honey. Perfect for a cold winter evening.

Boiling water	3 cups	750 mL
Orange pekoe tea bags	4	4
Apple juice	3 cups	750 mL
Liquid honey	1/3 cup	75 mL
Lemon juice	2 tbsp.	30 mL
Ice		

Pour boiling water into teapot. Add tea bags. Cover. Let steep for 5 minutes. Squeeze and discard tea bags.

Combine apple juice, honey and lemon juice in pitcher. Add tea. Stir. Cover. Chill for 4 to 6 hours until cold. Makes about 6 cups (1.5 L). Pour over ice in 4 large glasses. Serves 4.

1 serving: 203 Calories; 0.2 g Total Fat (0 g Mono, 0.1 g Poly, 0 g Sat); 0 mg Cholesterol; 53 g Carbohydrate; trace Fibre; 0 g Protein; 13 mg Sodium

Serving Suggestion: Garnish with slices of lemon or apple.

1. Maple Iced Coffee, page 27
2. Coffee Granita, page 28
3. Cinnamon Iced Coffee, page 26

Props Courtesy Of: Stokes
The Bay

Earl Grey Iced Tea

*Crisp, natural iced tea flavour with just
a hint of mint. A refreshing summer drink.*

Boiling water	8 cups	2 L
Granulated sugar	1/3 cup	75 mL
Lemon juice	1/4 cup	60 mL
Chopped fresh mint leaves	1/4 cup	60 mL
Earl Grey tea bags	4	4
Cinnamon sticks (4 inches, 10 cm, each)	2	2
Thin lemon slices	6	6
Ice		

Measure first 6 ingredients into large heatproof bowl. Stir until sugar is dissolved. Cover. Chill for at least 8 hours or overnight to blend flavours.

Strain tea mixture through sieve into pitcher. Discard solids. Add lemon slices. Stir. Makes about 7 cups (1.75 L). Pour over ice in 6 large glasses. Serves 6.

1 serving: 51 Calories; 0 g Total Fat (0 g Mono, 0 g Poly, 0 g Sat); 0 mg Cholesterol; 14 g Carbohydrate; 0 g Fibre; 0 g Protein; 10 mg Sodium

Pictured on page 54.

1. Honey Ginger Iced Tea, page 41
2. Queen Bee Sparkle, page 38
3. Spiced Chai Tea, page 39

Props Courtesy Of: Dansk Gifts
Pier 1 Imports
Stokes
The Bay

Queen Bee Sparkle

Golden yellow with a splash of licorice flavour.
It'll be the buzz of the party!

Boiling water	3 cups	750 mL
Green tea bags	3	3
Yellow-coloured, licorice-flavoured liqueur (such as Galliano), 4 oz. (see Note)	1/2 cup	125 mL
Lemon juice	1/4 cup	60 mL
Liquid honey	2 tbsp.	30 mL
Ginger ale	2 cups	500 mL
Lemon slices		
Ice		

Pour boiling water into teapot. Add tea bags. Cover. Let steep for 5 minutes. Squeeze and discard tea bags.

Combine liqueur, lemon juice and honey in pitcher. Add tea. Stir. Cover. Chill for 4 to 6 hours until cold.

Add ginger ale and lemon slices. Stir gently. Makes about 7 cups (1.75 L). Pour over ice in 6 large glasses. Serves 6.

1 serving: 143 Calories; 0.1 g Total Fat (0 g Mono, 0 g Poly, 0 g Sat); 0 mg Cholesterol; 24 g Carbohydrate; 0 g Fibre; 0 g Protein; 11 mg Sodium

Pictured on page 36.

Note: If you cannot find Galliano, add several drops of yellow liquid food colouring to same amount of clear licorice-flavoured liqueur (such as Sambuca) until desired shade is reached.

Serving Suggestion: Garnish with lemon wedge on glass.

Spiced Chai Tea

Caramel-coloured, mildly spiced East Indian tea. Delicious hot or cold.

Water	2 1/2 cups	625 mL
Thinly sliced, peeled gingerroot	2 tbsp.	30 mL
Fennel seed	1/2 tsp.	2 mL
Whole cloves	5	5
Whole black peppercorns	5	5
Whole green cardamom, bruised (see Tip, below)	5	5
Whole allspice	5	5
Orange pekoe tea bags	3	3
Vanilla bean, split (or 1 tsp., 5 mL, vanilla)	1	1
Milk	2 1/2 cups	625 mL
Liquid honey	3 tbsp.	50 mL

Combine first 9 ingredients in large saucepan. Bring to a boil on medium. Reduce heat to medium-low. Simmer, uncovered, for about 20 minutes until fragrant. Remove from heat. Strain through sieve into large bowl. Discard solids. Return tea mixture to same saucepan.

Add milk and honey. Stir well. Heat on medium until bubbles form around edge. Remove from heat. Makes about 4 cups (1 L). Pour into 4 small mugs. Serves 4.

1 serving: 121 Calories; 1.7 g Total Fat (0.5 g Mono, 0.1 g Poly, 1.1 g Sat); 6 mg Cholesterol; 21 g Carbohydrate; 0 g Fibre; 5 g Protein; 86 mg Sodium

Pictured on page 36.

CHOCOLATE CHAI: Omit milk. Use same amount of chocolate milk.

ICED SPICED CHAI: Chill Spiced Chai Tea. Pour over ice in large glasses or process with ice cubes in blender, using 3 to 4 ice cubes per serving.

 tip *To bruise cardamom, hit cardamom pods with mallet or flat side of wide knife to "bruise" or crack them open slightly.*

Brandy Tea Slush

*Sure to become a favourite. Apricot-coloured slush
with a mild, refreshing flavour.*

Boiling water	2 cups	500 mL
Orange pekoe tea bags	4	4
Water	7 cups	1.75 L
Granulated sugar	1 cup	250 mL
Apricot (or peach) brandy (16 oz.)	2 cups	500 mL
Can of frozen concentrated lemonade, thawed	12 1/2 oz.	355 mL
Can of frozen concentrated orange juice, thawed	12 1/2 oz.	355 mL
Ginger ale	12 cups	3 L

Pour boiling water into extra-large heatproof bowl. Add tea bags. Let steep for 10 minutes. Squeeze and discard tea bags.

Combine water and sugar in large saucepan. Bring to a boil on medium. Boil for about 1 minute, stirring occasionally, until sugar is dissolved. Remove from heat. Add to tea.

Add brandy and concentrated lemonade and orange juice. Stir well. Pour into large plastic container with tight-fitting lid (one 16 cup, 4 L, ice cream pail works well). Cover. Freeze until firm. Makes about 14 cups (3.5 L) slush.

Scoop slush into chilled large glasses until 2/3 full. Fill each with about 2/3 cup (150 mL) ginger ale. Serve with a straw and spoon. Serves 20.

1 serving: 222 Calories; 0.1 g Total Fat (0 g Mono, 0 g Poly, 0 g Sat); 0 mg Cholesterol; 43 g Carbohydrate; trace Fibre; 1 g Protein; 13 mg Sodium

Honey Ginger Iced Tea

Semi-sweet iced tea with a lemon and ginger snap!

Water	4 cups	1 L
Thinly sliced, peeled gingerroot	2 tbsp.	30 mL
Orange pekoe tea bags	3	3
Liquid honey	1/3 cup	75 mL
Lemon juice	2 tbsp.	30 mL
Ice		
Fresh mint sprigs, for garnish		

Combine water and ginger in medium saucepan. Bring to a boil on medium-high. Remove from heat.

Add tea bags. Let steep for 5 minutes. Strain through sieve into heatproof pitcher. Discard solids.

Add honey and lemon juice. Stir. Cover. Chill for 4 to 6 hours until cold. Makes about 4 cups (1 L).

Pour over ice in 4 large glasses. Garnish with mint sprigs. Serves 4.

1 serving: 111 Calories; 0 g Total Fat (0 g Mono, 0 g Poly, 0 g Sat); 0 mg Cholesterol; 30 g Carbohydrate; 0 g Fibre; 0 g Protein; 9 mg Sodium

Pictured on page 36.

Serving Suggestion: Serve over crushed ice for a sparkling presentation on a hot summer day.

Paré Pointer
Say cheers in French: "Santé!" (SAHN-tay)

Iced Pineapple Tea

Pleasantly sweet pineapple with a gentle ginger mist.

Can of frozen concentrated pineapple juice	12 1/2 oz.	355 mL
Cold strong prepared tea	3 cups	750 mL
Lemon juice	3 tbsp.	50 mL
Ginger ale	3 cups	750 mL

Ice

Combine concentrated pineapple juice, tea and lemon juice in pitcher. Add ginger ale. Stir gently. Makes about 7 1/2 cups (1.9 L).

Pour over ice in 6 large glasses. Serves 6.

1 serving: 177 Calories; 0.1 g Total Fat (0 g Mono, 0 g Poly, 0 g Sat); 0 mg Cholesterol; 45 g Carbohydrate; 0 g Fibre; 1 g Protein; 19 mg Sodium

Serving Suggestion: Place wedge of fresh pineapple (with peel) on edge of glass or thread canned pineapple tidbits alternating with maraschino cherries onto cocktail pick for garnish.

Orange Ginger Infusion

A tasty beverage any time, but especially calming when you have a head cold. It will have you feeling better in no time!

Water	3 1/2 cups	875 mL
Thinly sliced, peeled gingerroot	1/4 cup	60 mL
Frozen concentrated orange juice	1/4 cup	60 mL
Sweetened powdered orange-flavoured drink crystals	2 tbsp.	30 mL
Liquid honey (optional)	2 tsp.	10 mL

Combine first 4 ingredients in medium saucepan. Bring to a boil on medium. Reduce heat to medium-low. Simmer, uncovered, for about 5 minutes until fragrant. Remove from heat. Remove and discard ginger.

Add honey. Stir. Makes about 4 cups (1 L). Pour into 4 small mugs. Serves 4.

1 serving: 53 Calories; 0 g Total Fat (0 g Mono, 0 g Poly, 0 g Sat); 0 mg Cholesterol; 13 g Carbohydrate; trace Fibre; 0 g Protein; 2 mg Sodium

Chamomile Refresher

*Mild flavours of chamomile, pineapple and mint
in a refreshing, pale yellow tea.*

Boiling water	2 cups	500 mL
Chamomile tea bags	3	3
Fresh mint sprigs	2	2
Sparkling bottled water (such as Perrier)	1 1/2 cups	375 mL
Pineapple juice	1 cup	250 mL
White grape juice	1 cup	250 mL
Orange juice	1/2 cup	125 mL
Sweetened powdered lemon-flavoured drink crystals	2 – 3 tbsp.	30 – 50 mL
Ice		

Pour boiling water into heatproof medium bowl. Add tea bags and mint. Let steep for 10 minutes. Strain through sieve into pitcher. Discard solids.

Add next 5 ingredients. Stir until drink crystals are dissolved. Makes about 6 cups (1.5 L). Pour over ice in 4 large glasses. Serves 4.

1 serving: 122 Calories; 0.2 g Total Fat (0 g Mono, 0.1 g Poly, 0 g Sat); 0 mg Cholesterol; 30 g Carbohydrate; trace Fibre; 1 g Protein; 8 mg Sodium

Paré Pointer
Say cheers in German: "Proest!" (PROHST)

Cranberry Iced Tea

Cold cranberry and orange tea. Satisfying, thirst-quenching beverage.

Boiling water	3 cups	750 mL
Orange pekoe tea bags	5	5
Can of frozen concentrated cranberry cocktail	9 1/2 oz.	275 mL
Orange juice	1 cup	250 mL
Fresh (or frozen, thawed) cranberries	3 tbsp.	50 mL
Thin orange slices, halved	4	4
Ice		

Pour boiling water into teapot. Add tea bags. Cover. Let steep for 5 minutes. Squeeze and discard tea bags.

Combine concentrated cranberry cocktail and orange juice in pitcher. Add tea. Stir. Cover. Chill for 4 to 6 hours until cold. Makes 5 cups (1.25 L).

Add cranberries and orange slice halves. Stir.

Pour over ice in 4 large glasses. Serves 4.

1 serving: 191 Calories; 0.1 g Total Fat (0 g Mono, 0 g Poly, 0 g Sat); 0 mg Cholesterol; 48 g Carbohydrate; trace Fibre; 1 g Protein; 9 mg Sodium

CRANBERRY TEA SPRITZER: Pour Cranberry Iced Tea into large glasses until 1/2 to 2/3 full. Fill with ginger ale, club soda or sparkling bottled water (such as Perrier).

Mango Tea

Enjoy this fruity, hot drink. A refreshing break in your day.

Water	3 1/2 cups	875 mL
Can of frozen concentrated mango punch	12 1/2 oz.	355 mL
Almond-flavoured syrup (such as Torani's)	1 tbsp.	15 mL
Ground cinnamon	1/4 tsp.	1 mL
Orange pekoe tea bags	3 – 4	3 – 4

(continued on next page)

Combine first 4 ingredients in medium saucepan. Bring to a boil on medium. Remove from heat.

Add tea bags. Cover. Let steep for 5 minutes. Squeeze and discard tea bags. Makes about 5 cups (1.25 L). Pour into 4 large mugs. Serves 4.

1 serving: 203 Calories; 0.8 g Total Fat (0.1 g Mono, 0.2 g Poly, 0.1 g Sat); 0 mg Cholesterol; 50 g Carbohydrate; 0 g Fibre; 0 g Protein; 20 mg Sodium

Variation (with alcohol): Omit almond-flavoured syrup. Use same amount of almond-flavoured liqueur (such as Amaretto).

Serving Suggestion: Garnish with cinnamon sticks.

Sweet Spiced Tea

Mildly spiced, sweet and satisfying. Good hot or cold.

Water	6 cups	1.5 L
Granulated sugar	1/4 – 1/3 cup	60 – 75 mL
Whole green cardamom, bruised (see Tip, page 39)	4	4
Whole cloves	4	4
Cinnamon stick (4 inches, 10 cm)	1	1
Orange pekoe tea bags	3	3

Heat and stir first 5 ingredients in medium saucepan on medium-high until sugar is dissolved. Bring to a boil. Remove from heat. Let stand for 15 minutes.

Add tea bags. Bring to a boil on medium-high. Reduce heat to medium-low. Simmer, uncovered, for 3 minutes. Remove from heat. Strain through sieve into teapot. Discard solids. Makes about 5 cups (1.25 L). Pour into 4 large mugs. Serves 4.

1 serving: 53 Calories; 0 g Total Fat (0 g Mono, 0 g Poly, 0 g Sat); 0 mg Cholesterol; 14 g Carbohydrate; 0 g Fibre; 0 g Protein; 6 mg Sodium

Serving Suggestion: Add a fresh cinnamon stick to your cup of tea for extra spice.

Banana Egg Flip

Creamy white and frothy. A nourishing combination in a delicious milkshake!

Milk	2 cups	500 mL
Vanilla ice cream	1 cup	250 mL
Plain yogurt	3 tbsp.	50 mL
Liquid honey	2 tbsp.	30 mL
Ripe medium banana, cut up	1	1
Large egg (see Note)	1	1
Ice cubes	3	3

Process all 7 ingredients in blender until smooth. Makes about 4 1/2 cups (1.1 L). Pour into 4 chilled medium glasses. Serves 4.

1 serving: 209 Calories; 6.8 g Total Fat (2 g Mono, 0.4 g Poly, 3.8 g Sat); 75 mg Cholesterol; 31 g Carbohydrate; trace Fibre; 8 g Protein; 117 mg Sodium

Note: Eggs used in beverages should be cold. Remove egg from refrigerator just before adding. Beverages containing uncooked egg should be served immediately.

Peanut Butter Blast

Familiar flavour combination—peanut butter, chocolate and banana—in a breakfast or snack beverage.

Milk	1 1/2 cups	375 mL
Chocolate ice cream	1 cup	250 mL
Frozen ripe medium banana (see Tip, page 21)	1	1
Smooth (or crunchy) peanut butter	1 tbsp.	15 mL

Process all 4 ingredients in blender until smooth. Makes about 3 1/2 cups (875 mL). Pour into 4 chilled small glasses. Serves 4.

1 serving: 167 Calories; 7.1 g Total Fat (2.4 g Mono, 0.8 g Poly, 3.5 g Sat); 16 mg Cholesterol; 22 g Carbohydrate; 1 g Fibre; 6 g Protein; 94 mg Sodium

Pictured on page 53.

Apple Ginger Mocktail

Light, carbonated drink with a crisp, clean taste. Sweet and tangy.

Apple juice	1 cup	250 mL
Lemon juice	1 tbsp.	15 mL
Grenadine syrup	1 tsp.	5 mL
Crushed ice		
Ginger ale	1 1/2 cups	375 mL

Combine apple juice, lemon juice and grenadine in 2 cup (500 mL) liquid measure. Pour over crushed ice in 2 medium glasses.

Slowly add ginger ale until full. Stir gently. Makes about 2 1/2 cups (625 mL). Serves 2.

1 serving: 140 Calories; 0.1 g Total Fat (0 g Mono, 0 g Poly, 0 g Sat); 0 mg Cholesterol; 36 g Carbohydrate; trace Fibre; 0 g Protein; 20 mg Sodium

Serving Suggestion: Garnish with thin apple slices.

Rainbow Floats

Sweet and fruity with a fun, foamy rainbow top. Kids will love it!

Lemon lime soft drink	1 cup	250 mL
Cranberry cocktail	1/2 cup	125 mL
Rainbow sherbet	1 cup	250 mL

Pour lemon lime soft drink and cranberry cocktail into 2 chilled large glasses. Stir gently.

Carefully add 1/2 cup (125 mL) sherbet (about 2 scoops) to each glass. Mixture will foam. Makes about 3 cups (750 mL). Serves 2.

1 serving: 230 Calories; 2.1 g Total Fat (0.5 g Mono, 0.1 g Poly, 1.2 g Sat); 5 mg Cholesterol; 54 g Carbohydrate; 0 g Fibre; 1 g Protein; 62 mg Sodium

Pictured on page 53.

Serving Suggestion: Add a straw and spoon so kids of all ages will be able to enjoy this drink to the last drop!

Grape Lemonade

This pink punch gets more purple as the grape-flavoured ice cubes melt. Cold, sweet and tart.

Can of frozen concentrated grape juice, thawed	12 oz.	341 mL
Water	1 1/2 cups	375 mL
Can of frozen concentrated pineapple juice, partially thawed	12 1/2 oz.	355 mL
Frozen concentrated lemonade, partially thawed	1/2 cup	125 mL
Grenadine syrup	1 tbsp.	15 mL
Water	5 cups	1.25 L

Lemon slices, for garnish

Combine concentrated grape juice and water in 4 cup (1 L) liquid measure. Pour into ice cube trays. Freeze until firm. Makes about 24 cubes.

Combine next 4 ingredients in small punch bowl. Add frozen grape juice cubes. Makes about 9 1/2 cups (2.4 L).

Garnish with lemon slices. Serves 10.

1 serving: 189 Calories; 0.2 g Total Fat (0 g Mono, 0.1 g Poly, 0.1 g Sat); 0 mg Cholesterol; 47 g Carbohydrate; trace Fibre; 1 g Protein; 6 mg Sodium

Pictured on page 53.

 At the peak of melon season, chop watermelon into bite-size pieces. Freeze in single layer on ungreased baking sheet. Store in resealable freezer bags for up to 12 months. Use in a variety of beverages. Enjoy a taste of summer in the middle of winter!

Kids' Drinks

Watermelon Slush

Kids and adults will love this on a hot day.
Yummy and fun—the ginger ale tickles the tongue.

Chopped seedless watermelon (see Tip, page 48)	3 cups	750 mL
Can of frozen concentrated white grape cocktail, partially thawed	12 oz.	341 mL
Ginger ale	6 cups	1.5 L

Process watermelon and concentrated grape cocktail in blender until smooth. Pour into 2 quart (2 L) shallow baking dish. Cover. Freeze for about 2 hours until almost firm. Makes about 3 3/4 cups (925 mL) slush.

Scrape about 2/3 cup (150 mL) slush, using fork, into each of 6 chilled large glasses. Slowly add ginger ale until full. Stir gently. Serves 6.

1 serving: 239 Calories; 0.6 g Total Fat (0 g Mono, 0.1 g Poly, 0.1 g Sat); 0 mg Cholesterol; 59 g Carbohydrate; 1 g Fibre; 1 g Protein; 25 mg Sodium

Serving Suggestion: Garnish each glass with small slice of watermelon and fresh strawberry.

Peach Dream

Lightly flavoured peach drink with a subtle hint of orange.

Milk	2 1/2 cups	625 mL
Can of sliced peaches (with juice)	14 oz.	398 mL
Vanilla ice cream	1 cup	250 mL
Orange juice	1/3 cup	75 mL
Vanilla	1/4 tsp.	1 mL
Ice cubes		

Process first 5 ingredients in blender until smooth. Makes about 6 2/3 cups (1.65 L). Pour over ice cubes in 6 chilled medium glasses. Serves 6.

1 serving: 129 Calories; 3.8 g Total Fat (1.1 g Mono, 0.2 g Poly, 2.3 g Sat); 15 mg Cholesterol; 20 g Carbohydrate; 1 g Fibre; 5 g Protein; 75 mg Sodium

Apple "Moose"

A "moose" you can drink!
This frothy mousse tastes like apple pie and ice cream.

Vanilla ice cream	1 cup	250 mL
Milk	1 cup	250 mL
Unsweetened applesauce	1/4 cup	60 mL
Lemon juice	1 tsp.	5 mL

Process all 4 ingredients in blender until smooth. Makes about 2 1/3 cups (575 mL). Pour into 2 chilled medium glasses. Serves 2.

1 serving: 209 Calories; 9.1 g Total Fat (2.6 g Mono, 0.3 g Poly, 5.6 g Sat); 36 mg Cholesterol; 27 g Carbohydrate; 1 g Fibre; 7 g Protein; 121 mg Sodium

Serving Suggestion: Serve with a straw. Top with candy sprinkles just for fun!

Just Peachy

Refreshing peach flavour.

Peach nectar	1/2 cup	125 mL
Orange juice	1/3 cup	75 mL
Lemon juice	2 tsp.	10 mL
Crushed ice	1/4 cup	60 mL
Lemon lime soft drink (or ginger ale)	1/2 cup	125 mL

Combine first 3 ingredients in 1 cup (250 mL) liquid measure.

Measure crushed ice into chilled large glass. Pour peach mixture over top. Slowly add lemon lime soft drink until full. Stir gently. Makes about 1 2/3 cups (400 mL). Serves 1.

1 serving: 165 Calories; 0.2 g Total Fat (0 g Mono, 0.1 g Poly, 0 g Sat); 0 mg Cholesterol; 42 g Carbohydrate; 1 g Fibre; 1 g Protein; 24 mg Sodium

Serving Suggestion: Garnish with thin slice of fresh peach. Use club soda in place of soft drink for a less sweet alternative.

Frosty Mandarin

Rich, cold orange cream.

Can of mandarin orange segments (with juice)	10 oz.	284 mL
Vanilla ice cream (or frozen yogurt)	1 cup	250 mL
Orange sherbet	1/2 cup	125 mL

Process all 3 ingredients in blender until smooth. Makes about 2 1/2 cups (625 mL). Pour into 2 chilled medium glasses. Serves 2.

1 serving: 265 Calories; 8.7 g Total Fat (2.5 g Mono, 0.3 g Poly, 5.3 g Sat); 33 mg Cholesterol; 46 g Carbohydrate; 1 g Fibre; 4 g Protein; 87 mg Sodium

Pictured on page 53.

Midnight Punch

Sweet purple punch kids will love. Great to serve at a party.

Club soda	8 cups	2 L
Granulated sugar	1 cup	250 mL
Envelope of unsweetened powdered grape-flavoured drink crystals	1/4 oz.	6 g
Envelope of unsweetened powdered orange-flavoured drink crystals	1/4 oz.	6 g
Ginger ale	8 cups	2 L

Combine first 4 ingredients in small punch bowl. Stir gently until sugar is dissolved.

Add ginger ale. Stir gently. Makes about 16 cups (4 L). Serves 16.

1 serving: 95 Calories; 0 g Total Fat (0 g Mono, 0 g Poly, 0 g Sat); 0 mg Cholesterol; 24 g Carbohydrate; 0 g Fibre; 0 g Protein; 36 mg Sodium

Serving Suggestion: For a spooky effect at Halloween, fill 2 plastic gloves with water, secure tightly and freeze until firm. Carefully peel or cut away gloves and place frozen "hands" in punch bowl.

Pink Moo Juice

Strawberry flavour in a satisfying, creamy beverage.
Add more ice cream topping or yogurt if you prefer a sweeter taste.

Milk	2 cups	500 mL
Frozen whole strawberries, chopped	1 cup	250 mL
Strawberry ice cream topping (or jam)	1/4 cup	60 mL
Fresh strawberries, for garnish	4	4

Process first 3 ingredients in blender until smooth. Makes about 3 3/4 cups (925 mL). Pour into 4 chilled small glasses.

Garnish each with fresh strawberry. Serves 4.

1 serving: 132 Calories; 1.5 g Total Fat (0.4 g Mono, 0.1 g Poly, 0.9 g Sat); 5 mg Cholesterol; 27 g Carbohydrate; 1 g Fibre; 5 g Protein; 70 mg Sodium

Variation: Omit milk. Use same amount of plain or flavoured yogurt for a thicker drink.

1. Rainbow Floats, page 47
2. Frosty Mandarin, page 51
3. Grape Lemonade, page 48
4. Peanut Butter Blast, page 46

Props Courtesy Of: Cherison Enterprises Inc.
Wal-Mart Canada Inc.
Zellers

Hot Chocolate For Two

A great winter warm-up for the kids after school
or at the end of a day playing in the snow.

Cocoa, sifted if lumpy	1 tbsp.	15 mL
Granulated sugar	1 tbsp.	15 mL
Water	3/4 cup	175 mL
Skim evaporated milk	3/4 cup	175 mL
Vanilla	3/4 tsp.	4 mL

Miniature marshmallows, for garnish

Combine cocoa and sugar in small cup. Divide and spoon into 2 small mugs.

Combine water, evaporated milk and vanilla in 2 cup (500 mL) liquid measure. Microwave on high (100%) for about 2 minutes until boiling. Pour into mugs. Stir until smooth. Makes about 1 1/2 cups (375 mL).

Garnish with marshmallows. Serves 2.

1 serving: 106 Calories; 0.5 g Total Fat (0.2 g Mono, 0 g Poly, 0.3 g Sat); 3 mg Cholesterol; 18 g Carbohydrate; 1 g Fibre; 7 g Protein; 107 mg Sodium

1. Pink Summer Slush, page 58
2. Earl Grey Iced Tea, page 37
3. Citrus Sunburst, page 68

Props Courtesy Of: Danesco Inc.
  Dansk Gifts
  Pier 1 Imports

Fruit Salad Chiller

This cold, fruity drink will give you the chills! Sweet, creamy cantaloupe flavour.

Vanilla ice cream	1 cup	250 mL
Sliced fresh strawberries	1/2 cup	125 mL
Sliced ripe banana	1/2 cup	125 mL
Chopped cantaloupe	1/2 cup	125 mL
Liquid honey	2 – 3 tbsp.	30 – 50 mL
Ice cubes	3	3

Process all 6 ingredients in blender until smooth. Makes about 2 cups (500 mL). Pour into 2 chilled medium glasses. Serves 2.

1 serving: 259 Calories; 8.1 g Total Fat (2.3 g Mono, 0.4 g Poly, 4.8 g Sat); 31 mg Cholesterol; 47 g Carbohydrate; 2 g Fibre; 3 g Protein; 61 mg Sodium

Serving Suggestion: Garnish each glass with a fresh strawberry.

Malted Milkshake

This is so frothy, it will make a great moustache!

Chocolate ice cream	2 cups	500 mL
Milk	1 cup	250 mL
Chocolate syrup	2 tbsp.	30 mL
Malt drink mix (such as Ovaltine)	2 tbsp.	30 mL

Process all 4 ingredients in blender until smooth. Makes about 3 cups (750 mL). Pour into 3 chilled medium glasses. Serves 3.

1 serving: 290 Calories; 11.5 g Total Fat (3.4 g Mono, 0.4 g Poly, 7.1 g Sat); 35 mg Cholesterol; 44 g Carbohydrate; 0 g Fibre; 7 g Protein; 167 mg Sodium

MALTED BANANA SHAKE: Add 1 ripe medium banana, cut up, to other ingredients. Process until smooth.

Berry Shake Up

Pleasant purple pick-me-up! Adults will like this one too.

Strawberry ice cream	2 cups	500 mL
Milk	2 cups	500 mL
Frozen blueberries	3/4 cup	175 mL
Vanilla	1/2 tsp.	2 mL

Process all 4 ingredients in blender until smooth. Makes about 4 2/3 cups (1.15 L). Pour into 4 chilled medium glasses. Serves 4.

1 serving: 205 Calories; 7.4 g Total Fat (0.4 g Mono, 0.1 g Poly, 0.9 g Sat); 25 mg Cholesterol; 29 g Carbohydrate; 1 g Fibre; 7 g Protein; 107 mg Sodium

Serving Suggestion: Garnish with fresh blueberries threaded onto cocktail picks.

Purple Cow

A creamy banana and blueberry drink that's not overly sweet.

Milk	1 cup	250 mL
Frozen ripe medium banana (see Tip, page 21)	1	1
Frozen blueberries	1/3 cup	75 mL
Berry (or plain) yogurt	3 tbsp.	50 mL
Liquid honey	1 – 2 tbsp.	15 – 30 mL

Process all 5 ingredients in blender until smooth. Makes about 2 cups (500 mL). Pour into 2 chilled medium glasses. Serves 2.

1 serving: 177 Calories; 2.2 g Total Fat (0.5 g Mono, 0.1 g Poly, 1.2 g Sat); 7 mg Cholesterol; 36 g Carbohydrate; 2 g Fibre; 6 g Protein; 77 mg Sodium

Pictured on front cover.

Summer Slush

Slushy drink perfect for that summer barbecue or backyard party.

Pineapple juice	6 cups	1.5 L
Orange juice	6 cups	1.5 L
Water	6 cups	1.5 L
Can of frozen concentrated orange juice, thawed	12 1/2 oz.	355 mL
Can of frozen concentrated lemonade, thawed	12 1/2 oz.	355 mL
Ripe medium bananas, cut up	4	4
Container of frozen strawberries in syrup, thawed	15 oz.	425 g
Vodka (or gin), 26 oz.	3 cups	750 mL
Lemon lime soft drink	24 cups	6 L

Divide and measure first 5 ingredients into 2 large plastic containers with tight-fitting lids (two 16 cup, 4 L, ice cream pails work well). Stir.

Process bananas and strawberries with syrup in blender until smooth. Divide and add to juice mixture in each plastic container.

Add 1 1/2 cups (375 mL) vodka to each. Stir well. Cover. Freeze until firm. Makes about 27 cups (6.75 L) slush.

Scoop slush into chilled large glasses until 3/4 full. Slowly add lemon lime soft drink until full. Serves about 36.

1 serving: 221 Calories; 0.3 g Total Fat (0 g Mono, 0.1 g Poly, 0 g Sat); 0 mg Cholesterol; 44 g Carbohydrate; 1 g Fibre; 1 g Protein; 21 mg Sodium

KIDS' SLUSH: Omit alcohol. Slush will freeze more firmly, but can still be scooped into glasses. Fill with soft drink.

PINK SUMMER SLUSH: Omit lemon lime soft drink. Use same amount of cream soda for a sweeter, pink slush.

Pictured on page 54.

Serving Suggestion: Great to have on hand for summer company. Slush can be frozen for up to 1 month. Just scoop into glasses and add soft drink, a straw and a spoon.

Pink Margarita Slush

Cool, tangy and deliciously refreshing.

Can of frozen concentrated cranberry lemonade	12 1/2 oz.	355 mL
Tequila (6 oz.)	3/4 cup	175 mL
Orange-flavoured liqueur (such as Grand Marnier), 6 oz.	3/4 cup	175 mL
Ice cubes	20 – 24	20 – 24

Measure concentrated lemonade, tequila and liqueur into blender. Cover. Process, adding ice cubes 2 or 3 at a time through hole in blender lid, scraping down sides if necessary, until thick and slushy. Makes about 5 cups (1.25 L). Pour into 6 chilled small glasses. Serves 6.

1 serving: 261 Calories; 0.1 g Total Fat (0 g Mono, 0 g Poly, 0 g Sat); 0 mg Cholesterol; 35 g Carbohydrate; 0 g Fibre; 0 g Protein; 3 mg Sodium

Serving Suggestion: Dampen rims of margarita glasses (see page 8) with lemon wedge, or dip into lemon juice in saucer. Press rims into granulated sugar in separate saucer until coated. Fill glasses with slush. Garnish each with lemon wedge.

Fruity Yogurt Freeze

A drink that is thick enough to eat with a spoon until it starts to melt. Perfect on a hot summer day when you need to cool down!

Frozen whole strawberries, chopped	1 cup	250 mL
Pineapple tidbits (with juice), about 1/2 of 14 oz. (398 mL) can	3/4 cup	175 mL
Frozen ripe medium banana (see Tip, page 21)	1	1
Vanilla frozen yogurt	1/2 cup	125 mL
Vanilla	1/2 tsp.	2 mL

Process all 5 ingredients in blender until smooth. Makes about 3 cups (750 mL). Pour into 2 chilled large glasses. Serves 2.

1 serving: 217 Calories; 2.6 g Total Fat (0.7 g Mono, 0.2 g Poly, 1.4 g Sat); 1 mg Cholesterol; 49 g Carbohydrate; 4 g Fibre; 3 g Protein; 37 mg Sodium

Berry Citrus Freeze

Strawberry and orange-flavoured margarita with a lime tang. Not overly sweet.

Frozen whole strawberries, chopped	2 cups	500 mL
Orange juice	1 1/2 cups	375 mL
Strawberry ice cream topping	1/4 cup	60 mL
Lime juice	3 tbsp.	50 mL
Tequila (3 oz.)	6 tbsp.	100 mL
Orange-flavoured liqueur (such as Grand Marnier), 1 1/2 oz.	3 tbsp.	50 mL

Process first 4 ingredients in blender until smooth. Pour into 2 quart (2 L) shallow baking dish. Cover. Freeze for about 2 hours until almost firm.

Scrape strawberry mixture, using fork, into blender. Add tequila and liqueur. Process until smooth. Makes about 3 1/2 cups (875 mL). Pour into 4 chilled small glasses. Serves 4.

1 serving: 219 Calories; 0.4 g Total Fat (0.1 g Mono, 0.1 g Poly, 0 g Sat); 0 mg Cholesterol; 37 g Carbohydrate; 2 g Fibre; 1 g Protein; 9 mg Sodium

Pictured on page 108.

Serving Suggestion: To dress up this drink, dampen rims of glasses with lime wedge, or dip into lime juice in saucer. Press rims into coloured sugar in separate saucer until coated. Garnish each with half of a fresh strawberry.

Lemonade Shake

Refreshing lemonade in a shake—sure to be a favourite. Delicious!

Vanilla ice cream	2 cups	500 mL
Sparkling lemonade soft drink	1 cup	250 mL
Frozen concentrated pink lemonade (or lemonade), partially thawed	1/4 cup	60 mL

Process all 3 ingredients in blender until smooth. Makes about 2 2/3 cups (650 mL). Pour into 2 chilled medium glasses. Serves 2.

1 serving: 403 Calories; 15.4 g Total Fat (4.4 g Mono, 0.6 g Poly, 9.5 g Sat); 61 mg Cholesterol; 65 g Carbohydrate; 0 g Fibre; 5 g Protein; 117 mg Sodium

Banana Colada Cooler

Creamy, cold tropical drink with rich banana and coconut flavours.

Pineapple juice	2 cups	500 mL
Frozen ripe medium bananas (see Tip, page 21)	3	3
Can of coconut milk	14 oz.	398 mL
White (light) rum (5 oz.)	2/3 cup	150 mL

Pour pineapple juice into ice cube trays. Freeze for about 4 hours until firm.

Put 1/2 of frozen pineapple juice cubes into blender. Add 1 1/2 bananas, 1/2 can of coconut milk and 1/3 cup (75 mL) rum. Process until smooth. Transfer to large pitcher. Repeat with remaining juice cubes, bananas, coconut milk and rum. Makes about 7 cups (1.75 mL). Pour into 6 chilled medium glasses. Serves 6.

1 serving: 287 Calories; 13.9 g Total Fat (0.6 g Mono, 0.2 g Poly, 12.1 g Sat); 0 mg Cholesterol; 27 g Carbohydrate; 1 g Fibre; 2 g Protein; 10 mg Sodium

Peach Melba

Creamy milkshake fashioned after the classic dessert.
Sweet peach with tangy raspberry.

Can of sliced peaches (with juice)	14 oz.	398 mL
Vanilla ice cream	1 cup	250 mL
Milk	1/2 cup	125 mL
Raspberry jam	2 tbsp.	30 mL

Process all 4 ingredients in blender until smooth. Makes about 3 cups (750 mL). Pour into 2 chilled large glasses. Serves 2.

1 serving: 308 Calories; 8.5 g Total Fat (2.5 g Mono, 0.4 g Poly, 5.2 g Sat); 33 mg Cholesterol; 57 g Carbohydrate; 2 g Fibre; 6 g Protein; 104 mg Sodium

Serving Suggestion: Garnish with whipped topping mixed with almond flavouring. Top with a fresh raspberry for a splash of colour.

Raspberry Margarita

Brilliant raspberry-red refreshment. Yum!

Container of frozen raspberries in syrup, thawed	15 oz.	425 g
Lemon juice	1/4 cup	60 mL
Raspberry jam	3 tbsp.	50 mL
Tequila (2 oz.)	1/4 cup	60 mL
Orange-flavoured liqueur (such as Grand Marnier), 2 oz.	1/4 cup	60 mL
Crushed ice	1 cup	250 mL

Combine first 3 ingredients in medium bowl. Strain raspberry mixture through sieve into 1 quart (1 L) shallow baking dish. Discard seeds. Spread raspberry mixture evenly in baking dish. Cover. Freeze for about 3 hours until almost firm.

Scrape raspberry mixture, using fork, into blender. Add tequila, liqueur and crushed ice. Process until smooth. Makes about 3 3/4 cups (925 mL). Pour into 4 small chilled glasses. Serves 4.

1 serving: 218 Calories; 0.2 g Total Fat (0 g Mono, 0.1 g Poly, 0 g Sat); 0 mg Cholesterol; 39 g Carbohydrate; 5 g Fibre; 1 g Protein; 8 mg Sodium

Pictured on page 71.

Serving Suggestion: Dampen rims of margarita glasses (see page 8) with lemon wedge, or dip into lemon juice in saucer. Press rims into coloured sugar in separate saucer until coated.

Frozen Drinks

Orange Frostbite

Smooth and frothy—just right for the summer! Placing glasses in freezer
before serving will make this yummy drink even frostier!

Medium oranges, peeled, seeds and white pith removed	4	4
Vanilla ice cream	1 3/4 cups	425 mL
Orange Dream Liqueur, page 139 (or vodka), 4 oz. (optional)	1/2 cup	125 mL

Cut oranges into quarters. Place in blender.

Add ice cream and liqueur. Process until smooth. Makes about 4 cups (1 L). Pour into 4 chilled medium glasses. Serves 4.

1 serving (with alcohol): 266 Calories; 7.9 g Total Fat (2.3 g Mono, 0.3 g Poly, 4.8 g Sat); 31 mg Cholesterol; 41 g Carbohydrate; 2 g Fibre; 4 g Protein; 65 mg Sodium

Pictured on page 71.

Serving Suggestion: Use "glasses" made from whole oranges. Cut tops off large oranges about 1/4 of the way from stem end. Carefully cut around inside edge of orange to loosen. Remove fruit and juice to blender, using spoon, to use in recipe. Freeze shells for at least 2 hours until firm. Fill with drink. Add a short straw.

Paré Pointer
Say cheers in Greek: "Eis Igian!" (is-i EE-an)

Caesar Granita

Mildly spiced, icy Caesar. Stays cold until the last sip.

Clam tomato beverage (such as Clamato juice)	2 cups	500 mL
Vodka (2 oz.), optional	1/4 cup	60 mL
Lemon juice	1 tbsp.	15 mL
Worcestershire sauce	1/4 tsp.	1 mL
Celery salt	1/4 tsp.	1 mL
Hot pepper sauce	1/4 tsp.	1 mL
Pickled pepper rings, for garnish	2	2

Combine first 6 ingredients in medium bowl. Pour into 1 quart (1 L) shallow baking dish. Cover. Freeze for about 3 hours until almost firm. Makes about 2 2/3 cups (650 mL).

Scrape tomato mixture, using fork, into 2 chilled medium glasses. Garnish each with pepper ring. Serves 2.

1 serving (with alcohol): 189 Calories; 0.3 g Total Fat (0 g Mono, 0.1 g Poly, 0 g Sat); 0 mg Cholesterol; 29 g Carbohydrate; 0 g Fibre; 2 g Protein; 1200 mg Sodium

Bananarama

Velvety smooth, thick and creamy.

Vanilla ice cream	2 cups	500 mL
Brandy (1/2 oz.)	1 tbsp.	15 mL
Banana-flavoured liqueur (such as Crème de banane), 1/2 oz.	1 tbsp.	15 mL
Orange-flavoured liqueur (such as Grand Marnier), 1/4 oz.	1/2 tbsp.	7 mL

Grated chocolate (or chocolate curls), for garnish

Process first 4 ingredients in blender until smooth. Makes about 1 1/3 cups (325 mL). Pour into 2 chilled small glasses.

Sprinkle each with grated chocolate. Serves 2.

1 serving: 336 Calories; 15.4 g Total Fat (4.4 g Mono, 0.6 g Poly, 9.5 g Sat); 61 mg Cholesterol; 36 g Carbohydrate; 0 g Fibre; 5 g Protein; 112 mg Sodium

Tropical Daiquiri

Refreshing pineapple and coconut combination.
Half-and-half makes it creamier.

Fresh pineapple, cut into 1 inch (2.5 cm) cubes (or canned pineapple chunks, drained)	3 cups	750 mL
Milk (or half-and-half cream)	1 cup	250 mL
Crushed ice	1 cup	250 mL
Cream of coconut syrup	1/3 cup	75 mL
White (light) rum (2 1/2 oz.)	1/3 cup	75 mL
Maraschino cherries (with stems), for garnish	4	4

Spread pineapple cubes in single layer in 2 quart (2 L) shallow baking dish. Cover. Freeze for 2 to 3 hours until firm.

Measure next 4 ingredients into blender. Add 1/2 of frozen pineapple. Process until smooth. Add remaining pineapple. Process until smooth. Makes about 4 cups (1 L). Pour into 4 chilled medium glasses.

Garnish each with maraschino cherry. Serves 4.

1 serving: 182 Calories; 5.8 g Total Fat (0.5 g Mono, 0.3 g Poly, 4.5 g Sat); 3 mg Cholesterol; 20 g Carbohydrate; 2 g Fibre; 3 g Protein; 47 mg Sodium

Pictured on page 71.

Serving Suggestion: For a festive presentation, dampen rims of glasses with lemon wedge, or dip into lemon juice in small saucer. Press rims into coloured sugar in separate saucer until coated.

Paré Pointer
Say cheers in Hebrew: "L'chaim!" (le-HI-m)

Mocha Frappuccino

Slushy chocolate coffee—sweet and creamy.

Hot strong prepared coffee (see Note)	2 cups	500 mL
Brown sugar, packed	2 tbsp.	30 mL
Vanilla (or chocolate) ice cream, softened	1 cup	250 mL
Chocolate ice cream topping	1/4 cup	60 mL
Finely grated chocolate, for garnish	2 tbsp.	30 mL

Measure hot coffee and brown sugar into small bowl. Stir until sugar is dissolved. Pour into 1 quart (1 L) shallow baking dish. Cover. Freeze for about 3 hours until almost firm.

Scrape coffee mixture, using fork, into blender. Add ice cream and chocolate topping. Process until smooth. Makes about 2 2/3 cups (650 mL). Pour into 2 chilled medium glasses.

Sprinkle each with grated chocolate. Serves 2.

1 serving: 359 Calories; 13.7 g Total Fat (3.9 g Mono, 1.7 g Poly, 7.3 g Sat); 36 mg Cholesterol; 59 g Carbohydrate; 0 g Fibre; 5 g Protein; 130 mg Sodium

Note: For extra-strong flavour, use espresso.

Serving Suggestion: Add a straw to each glass for sipping.

Honeydew Granita

Processing it twice gives this granita a smooth texture. Superb!

Water	1 1/2 cups	375 mL
Granulated sugar	2/3 cup	150 mL
Chopped honeydew	3 cups	750 mL
Lemon juice	1 tbsp.	15 mL

Heat and stir water and sugar in medium saucepan on medium until sugar is dissolved. Increase heat to high. Bring to a boil. Boil, uncovered, for 3 minutes. Remove from heat. Cool.

Process sugar mixture, honeydew and lemon juice in blender until smooth. Pour into 2 quart (2 L) shallow baking dish. Cover. Freeze for about 4 hours until almost firm. Scrape mixture, using fork, into blender. Process until smooth. Makes about 5 cups (1.25 L). Pour into 4 chilled medium glasses. Serves 4.

1 serving: 185 Calories; 0.1 g Total Fat (0 g Mono, 0 g Poly, 0 g Sat); 0 mg Cholesterol; 48 g Carbohydrate; 1 g Fibre; 1 g Protein; 14 mg Sodium

Variation (with alcohol): Drizzle each with 2 to 3 tsp. (10 to 15 mL) melon-flavoured liqueur (such as Bols).

 To reduce the heat in chili peppers and jalapeño peppers, remove the seeds and ribs. Wear rubber gloves and avoid touching your eyes when handling hot peppers. Wash your hands well afterwards.

Citrus Sunburst

A refreshing, eye-catching drink, bursting with orange flavour.

CITRUS CREAM

Orange sherbet	2 cups	500 mL
Pink grapefruit juice	2/3 cup	150 mL
Can of mandarin orange segments (with juice)	10 oz.	284 mL
Ice cubes	6	6
Gin (3 oz.), optional	6 tbsp.	100 mL
Grenadine syrup	1/2 tsp.	2 mL
Lime slices, for garnish	4	4

Citrus Cream: Process first 4 ingredients in blender until smooth. Makes 3 1/2 cups (875 mL) cream.

Divide and measure gin and grenadine into 4 chilled small glasses. Pour Citrus Cream over top of each.

Garnish each with lime slice. Serves 4.

1 serving (with alcohol): 239 Calories; 2.1 g Total Fat (0.6 g Mono, 0.1 g Poly, 1.2 g Sat); 5 mg Cholesterol; 44 g Carbohydrate; trace Fibre; 2 g Protein; 52 mg Sodium

Pictured on page 54.

Paré Pointer
Say cheers in Icelandic: "Skal!" (SKOHL)

Watermelon Daiquiri

Thick and slushy watermelon with a splash of orange and lime.

Chopped seedless watermelon (see Tip, page 48)	4 cups	1 L
Lemon lime soft drink	3/4 cup	175 mL
White (light) rum (2 oz.)	1/4 cup	60 mL
Orange-flavoured liqueur (such as Grand Marnier), 2 oz.	1/4 cup	60 mL
Lime juice	3 tbsp.	50 mL

Spread watermelon in single layer in 2 quart (2 L) shallow baking dish. Cover. Freeze for about 3 hours until firm.

Place 1/2 of frozen watermelon in blender. Add next 4 ingredients. Process until smooth. Add remaining watermelon. Process until smooth. Makes about 4 cups (1 L). Pour into 4 chilled medium glasses. Serves 4.

1 serving: 145 Calories; 0.7 g Total Fat (0 g Mono, 0 g Poly, 0 g Sat); 0 mg Cholesterol; 18 g Carbohydrate; 1 g Fibre; 1 g Protein; 9 mg Sodium

Vanilla Malted

Tastes like chocolate malt balls, with a vanilla finish.
This one's sure to make you feel like a kid in a soda shop!

Vanilla ice cream	2 cups	500 mL
Sparkling bottled water (such as Perrier)	1/2 cup	125 mL
Malt drink mix (such as Ovaltine)	6 tbsp.	100 mL
Vanilla	1 1/2 tsp.	7 mL

Process all 4 ingredients in blender until just smooth. Do not over-process, as mixture thins quickly. Makes about 2 cups (500 mL). Pour into 2 chilled medium glasses. Serves 2.

1 serving: 346 Calories; 15.9 g Total Fat (4.6 g Mono, 0.6 g Poly, 9.8 g Sat); 62 mg Cholesterol; 47 g Carbohydrate; 0 g Fibre; 6 g Protein; 206 mg Sodium

CHOCOLATE MALTED: Omit vanilla ice cream. Use same amount of chocolate ice cream.

Serving Suggestion: Add a straw and sip to your heart's content.

Spiced Frozen Nog

Just when you thought eggnog couldn't get any better!
A cool holiday treat.

Vanilla ice cream	2 cups	500 mL
Eggnog	3/4 cup	175 mL
Ground cinnamon	1/8 tsp.	0.5 mL
Ground nutmeg	1/16 tsp.	0.5 mL
Ground ginger	1/16 tsp.	0.5 mL

Ground cinnamon (or nutmeg), sprinkle

Process first 5 ingredients in blender until smooth. Makes about 2 cups (500 mL). Pour into 2 chilled medium glasses.

Sprinkle each with cinnamon. Serves 2.

1 serving: 417 Calories; 22.9 g Total Fat (6.7 g Mono, 0.9 g Poly, 14 g Sat); 121 mg Cholesterol; 47 g Carbohydrate; trace Fibre; 9 g Protein; 167 mg Sodium

1. Raspberry Margarita, page 62
2. Tropical Daiquiri, page 65
3. Orange Frostbite, page 63

Props Courtesy Of: Pier 1 Imports

Frozen Drinks

Straw-Barb Juice

Strawberries and rhubarb were surely made for each other!

Fresh strawberries	1 1/2 cups	375 mL
Fresh rhubarb stalks, cut up	2	2
Liquid honey	2 tbsp.	30 mL
Ginger ale	1 cup	250 mL

Push strawberries and rhubarb through juicer feed chute. Discard pulp. Transfer juice to pitcher.

Add honey. Stir. Add ginger ale. Stir gently. Makes about 2 cups (500 mL). Pour into 2 medium glasses. Serves 2.

1 serving: 160 Calories; 0.5 g Total Fat (0 g Mono, 0.2 g Poly, 0 g Sat); 0 mg Cholesterol; 41 g Carbohydrate; 1 g Fibre; 1 g Protein; 13 mg Sodium

Pictured on page 72.

Serving Suggestion: Use other soft drink flavours, such as cream soda, lemon lime or club soda, for a new twist on this delicious combination.

1. Straw-Barb Juice, above
2. Fizzy Ale, page 74
3. Green Zinger, page 75
4. Orange Vegetable Brew, page 77

Props Courtesy Of: Pier 1 Imports
                    The Bay

Fizzy Ale

Good for what ails you! Delicious any time.

Large lemon wedge	1	1
Seedless green grapes	1 1/2 lbs.	680 g
Piece of peeled gingerroot (about 1/4 inch, 6 mm)	1	1
Sparkling bottled water (such as Perrier)	2 cups	500 mL
Ice		

Remove and discard thin layer of peel from lemon, leaving white pith on fruit. Push through juicer feed chute.

Push grapes and gingerroot through chute. Discard pulp. Transfer juice to pitcher.

Add sparkling water. Stir gently. Makes about 3 3/4 cups (925 mL).

Pour over ice in 4 medium glasses. Serves 4.

1 serving: 109 Calories; 0.6 g Total Fat (0 g Mono, 0.2 g Poly, 0.2 g Sat); 0 mg Cholesterol; 30 g Carbohydrate; trace Fibre; 1 g Protein; 5 mg Sodium

Pictured on page 72.

Serving Suggestion: Thread 2 grapes onto cocktail pick and place on side of each glass for garnish.

Winter Veggies Drink

Not getting enough veggies? Here's an answer.

Small yellow turnip, cut up	1	1
Small parsnips	6	6
Medium carrots	4	4

Push all 3 vegetables through juicer feed chute. Discard pulp. Makes about 1 2/3 cups (400 mL). Pour into 2 small glasses. Serves 2.

1 serving: 257 Calories; 1.1 g Total Fat (0.3 g Mono, 0.3 g Poly, 0.2 g Sat); 0 mg Cholesterol; 61 g Carbohydrate; 3 g Fibre; 5 g Protein; 121 mg Sodium

Green Zinger

Bright green, with fresh-from-the-garden flavour.

Medium zucchini (with peel), cut up	1	1
English cucumber (with peel), cut up	1	1
Small apple (with peel), core removed, cut up	1	1
Fresh whole green beans	1 cup	250 mL
Fresh pea pods	1 cup	250 mL
Fresh parsley sprigs	3	3
Fresh spinach leaves	15	15
Large dark green lettuce leaves	4	4

Push first 5 ingredients through juicer feed chute.

Roll parsley tightly in spinach and lettuce leaves. Push through chute. Discard pulp. Makes about 1 2/3 cups (400 mL). Pour into 2 small glasses. Serves 2.

1 serving: 126 Calories; 0.9 g Total Fat (0.1 g Mono, 0.4 g Poly, 0.2 g Sat); 0 mg Cholesterol; 27 g Carbohydrate; 1 g Fibre; 7 g Protein; 45 mg Sodium

Pictured on page 72.

Tropical Breeze

Delicious tropical flavour. Sunshine in a glass!

Medium mango, peeled and pitted, cut up	1	1
Medium papaya, peeled and seeds removed, cut up	1/2	1/2
Fresh pineapple slices (1/2 inch, 12 mm, thick), core removed	2	2

Push all 3 fruits through juicer feed chute. Discard pulp. Makes about 2 1/3 cups (575 mL). Pour into 2 medium glasses. Serves 2.

1 serving: 142 Calories; 0.8 g Total Fat (0.2 g Mono, 0.2 g Poly, 0.1 g Sat); 0 mg Cholesterol; 36 g Carbohydrate; 1 g Fibre; 1 g Protein; 5 mg Sodium

Pictured on page 90.

Serving Suggestion: Serve over ice, with a splash of club soda for sparkle.

Fruit Punch

Pretty pink, frothy refreshment.

Cantaloupe, seeds removed, cut up	1/2	1/2
Small apple (with peel), core removed, cut up	1	1
Fresh strawberries, cut up	6	6
Seedless red (or green) grapes	1/2 cup	125 mL
Fresh cranberries	1/2 cup	125 mL

Push all 5 fruits through juicer feed chute. Discard pulp (see Serving Suggestion). Makes about 1 1/2 cups (375 mL). Pour into 2 small glasses. Serves 2.

1 serving: 117 Calories; 0.8 g Total Fat (0 g Mono, 0.2 g Poly, 0.1 g Sat); 0 mg Cholesterol; 29 g Carbohydrate; 1 g Fibre; 2 g Protein; 13 mg Sodium

Serving Suggestion: To make a thicker drink, add small amount of pulp to juice. Stir.

Spicy Veggie Brew

You can substitute a few drops of hot pepper sauce for the chili pepper to spice up this juice to your taste.

Medium roma (plum) tomatoes, cut up	4	4
Small head of broccoli, cut up	1	1
Large orange (or red) pepper, cut up	1	1
English cucumber (with peel), cut up	1/2	1/2
Medium carrots, cut up	2	2
Celery ribs, cut up	2	2
Small fresh chili pepper, seeds and ribs removed (see Tip, page 67)	1	1

Push all 7 vegetables through juicer feed chute. Discard pulp. Makes about 2 cups (500 mL). Pour into 2 medium glasses. Serves 2.

1 serving: 167 Calories; 1.7 g Total Fat (0.2 g Mono, 0.8 g Poly, 0.3 g Sat); 0 mg Cholesterol; 37 g Carbohydrate; 2 g Fibre; 8 g Protein; 120 mg Sodium

Orange Vegetable Brew

Subtle and sweet flavours blend well in this brightly coloured brew.

Medium carrots, cut up	8	8
Celery ribs, cut up	3	3
Medium sweet potato (or yam), about 12 oz. (340 g), peeled and cut up	1	1
Acorn (or banana) squash, peeled and seeds removed, cut up	1	1

Push all 4 vegetables through juicer feed chute. Discard pulp. Makes about 2 1/4 cups (550 mL). Pour into 2 medium glasses. Serves 2.

1 serving: 251 Calories; 0.9 g Total Fat (0.1 g Mono, 0.4 g Poly, 0.2 g Sat); 0 mg Cholesterol; 61 g Carbohydrate; 2 g Fibre; 5 g Protein; 138 mg Sodium

Pictured on page 72.

Serving Suggestion: Add celery rib to each glass for the perfect stir stick!

Orchard Juice

Good rich flavour. Add enough honey to make as sweet as you like.

Medium apples (with peel), core removed, cut up	3	3
Fresh black (or red) plums, pitted	4	4
Fresh pears (with peel), core removed, cut up	3	3
Fresh apricots, pitted, cut up	3	3
Nectarines (or fresh peaches), pitted, cut up	2	2
Liquid honey (optional)	1 – 2 tbsp.	15 – 30 mL

Push all 5 fruits through juicer feed chute, alternating apple pieces with softer fruits. Discard pulp. Makes about 3 1/2 cups (875 mL). Transfer juice to pitcher. Juice will be foamy and will settle into layers.

Add honey. Stir well. Pour into 4 small glasses. Serve immediately. Serves 4.

1 serving: 169 Calories; 1.1 g Total Fat (0.3 g Mono, 0.2 g Poly, 0.1 g Sat); 0 mg Cholesterol; 43 g Carbohydrate; 1 g Fibre; 2 g Protein; 4 mg Sodium

Almond Soda

Lightly sweet almond flavour with a delicate lime zing.
A great choice for a hot summer's day.

Ice cubes	3	3
Almond-flavoured syrup (such as Torani's)	2 tbsp.	30 mL
Lime juice	2 tsp.	10 mL
Club soda	1 cup	250 mL
Lime slice, for garnish	1	1

Put ice cubes into medium glass. Add almond syrup, lime juice and club soda. Stir gently. Makes about 1 cup (250 mL).

Garnish with lime slice. Serves 1.

1 serving: 131 Calories; 0 g Total Fat (0 g Mono, 0 g Poly, 0 g Sat); 0 mg Cholesterol; 35 g Carbohydrate; trace Fibre; 0 g Protein; 83 mg Sodium

ALMOND SPRITZER: Omit almond-flavoured syrup. Use same amount (30 mL, 1 oz.) of almond-flavoured liqueur (such as Amaretto).

Cran-Almond Delight

Crisp cranberry with a delicate almond accent.

Crushed ice	1/4 cup	60 mL
Cranberry cocktail	3/4 cup	175 mL
Almond-flavoured liqueur (such as Amaretto), 1 oz.	2 tbsp.	30 mL
Club soda	1/4 cup	60 mL

Measure crushed ice into large glass. Add cranberry cocktail, liqueur and club soda. Stir gently. Makes about 1 1/4 cups (300 mL). Serves 1.

1 serving: 241 Calories; 0.3 g Total Fat (0 g Mono, 0.1 g Poly, 0.1 g Sat); 0 mg Cholesterol; 43 g Carbohydrate; 0 g Fibre; 0 g Protein; 19 mg Sodium

Pictured on page 108.

Variation (without alcohol): Omit liqueur. Use same amount of almond-flavoured syrup (such as Torani's).

Spicy Caesar

A popular drink. Spices can be increased
or decreased according to personal taste.

Clam tomato beverage (such as Clamato juice)	3 cups	750 mL
Vodka (4 oz.)	1/2 cup	125 mL
Prepared horseradish	1/2 – 1 tsp.	2 – 5 mL
Hot pepper sauce	1/2 tsp.	2 mL
Worcestershire Sauce	1/2 tsp.	2 mL
Ice		
Pickled asparagus spears, for garnish	4	4
Small lemon (or lime) wedges, for garnish	4	4

Measure first 5 ingredients into 4 cup (1 L) liquid measure. Stir. Makes about 3 1/2 cups (875 mL). Pour over ice in 4 medium glasses.

Garnish each with asparagus spear. Place lemon wedge on rim of each glass. Serves 4.

1 serving: 157 Calories; 0.2 g Total Fat (0 g Mono, 0 g Poly, 0 g Sat); 0 mg Cholesterol; 21 g Carbohydrate; trace Fibre; 1 g Protein; 775 mg Sodium

VIRGIN SPICY CAESAR: Omit vodka.

SPICY BLOODY MARY: Omit clam tomato beverage. Use same amount of tomato juice.

SALT AND PEPPER CAESAR: Omit vodka. Use same amount of Peppercorn Vodka, page 149.

Serving Suggestion: Dampen rims of glasses with lemon (or lime) wedge, or dip into lemon (or lime) juice in saucer. Press rims into celery salt in separate saucer until coated.

Banana Froster

*The classic Bananas Foster dessert is banana sautéed in rum
and brown sugar, served over vanilla ice cream. In this "Froster,"
these flavours are now in a glass. Yum!*

Half-and-half cream (or milk)	1/4 cup	60 mL
Banana-flavoured liqueur (such as Crème de banane), 1 oz.	2 tbsp.	30 mL
Dark (navy) rum (1/4 oz.)	1/2 tbsp.	7 mL
Brown sugar, packed	1 tsp.	5 mL
Crushed ice	1/4 cup	60 mL

Measure first 4 ingredients into cocktail shaker. Add crushed ice. Replace lid. Hold firmly and shake vigorously until cold and sugar is dissolved. Strain through sieve into small glass. Makes about 1/2 cup (125 mL). Serves 1.

1 serving: 236 Calories; 6.6 g Total Fat (1.9 g Mono, 0.3 g Poly, 4 g Sat); 20 mg Cholesterol; 22 g Carbohydrate; 0 g Fibre; 2 g Protein; 30 mg Sodium

Serving Suggestion: For a delectable difference, dampen rim of glass with lemon wedge, or dip into lemon juice in saucer. Press into brown sugar in separate saucer until coated.

Granny Smith

Slightly tart apple flavour with a citrus finish. Pucker up!

Ice cubes	3	3
Apple juice	1/4 cup	60 mL
Sour apple-flavoured liqueur (such as Sour Puss), 3/4 oz.	1 1/2 tbsp.	25 mL
Vodka (1/4 oz.)	1/2 tbsp.	7 mL
Sparkling lemonade (or lemonade)	1/2 cup	125 mL

Put ice cubes into medium glass. Add remaining 4 ingredients. Stir gently. Makes about 1 cup (250 mL). Serves 1.

1 serving: 149 Calories; 0.1 g Total Fat (0 g Mono, 0 g Poly, 0 g Sat); 0 mg Cholesterol; 21 g Carbohydrate; trace Fibre; 0 g Protein; 6 mg Sodium

Pictured on page 108.

Brandy Alexandra

A sister to "Brandy Alexander." Made with milk for a light, creamy cocktail.

Milk	3/4 cup	175 mL
Brandy (1 oz.)	2 tbsp.	30 mL
Chocolate-flavoured liqueur (such as Crème de cacao), 1/2 oz.	1 tbsp.	15 mL
Ice cubes	2 – 4	2 – 4

Ground nutmeg, sprinkle

Measure first 3 ingredients into cocktail shaker. Add ice cubes. Replace lid. Hold firmly and shake vigorously until cold. Strain through sieve into small glass. Makes about 1 cup (250 mL).

Sprinkle with nutmeg. Serves 1.

1 serving: 198 Calories; 4.5 g Total Fat (1.3 g Mono, 0.2 g Poly, 2.8 g Sat); 10 mg Cholesterol; 13 g Carbohydrate; 0 g Fibre; 7 g Protein; 112 mg Sodium

Serving Suggestion: To make this drink extra-special, dip rim of martini glass (see page 8) into melted chocolate in saucepan. Let stand until set.

Cold Buttered Rum

Indulge yourself with this creamy butterscotch treat.

Milk	2/3 cup	150 mL
Vanilla ice cream	1/2 cup	125 mL
Butterscotch ice cream topping	3 tbsp.	50 mL
Spiced rum (1 oz.)	2 tbsp.	30 mL
Ice		

Process first 4 ingredients in blender until smooth. Makes about 1 1/2 cups (375 mL). Pour over ice in 2 small glasses. Serves 2.

1 serving: 217 Calories; 4.8 g Total Fat (1.4 g Mono, 0.2 g Poly, 3 g Sat); 19 mg Cholesterol; 33 g Carbohydrate; 0 g Fibre; 5 g Protein; 180 mg Sodium

Variation (without alcohol): Omit spiced rum. Use 1/2 tsp. (2 mL) rum flavouring.

Cran-Razz Soda

Tangy, berry-flavoured soda, just sweet enough to satisfy. Exhilarating!

Cranberry cocktail	1/2 cup	125 mL
Raspberry-flavoured syrup (such as Torani's)	1/4 cup	60 mL
Can of club soda	12 1/2 oz.	355 mL
Ice		

Combine cranberry cocktail and raspberry syrup in 4 cup (1 L) liquid measure. Add club soda. Stir gently. Makes about 3 cups (750 mL). Pour over ice in 2 large glasses. Serves 2.

1 serving: 172 Calories; 0.1 g Total Fat (0 g Mono, 0 g Poly, 0 g Sat); 0 mg Cholesterol; 45 g Carbohydrate; 0 g Fibre; 0 g Protein; 70 mg Sodium

Pictured on page 89.

CRAN-RAZZ COCKTAIL: Add 1/4 cup (60 mL, 2 oz.) vodka to first 3 ingredients. Stir gently. Makes about 3 1/4 cups (800 mL). Serves 2.

Ginger "Ale"

Strong ginger and mild apple flavours come together in this sparkling, lime-coloured drink.

Crushed ice	1/4 cup	60 mL
Apple juice	1/2 cup	125 mL
Sour apple-flavoured liqueur (such as Sour Puss), 1 oz.	2 tbsp.	30 mL
Irish whiskey (1/4 oz.)	1/2 tbsp.	7 mL
Ginger beer	1/2 cup	125 mL

Measure crushed ice into large glass. Add remaining 4 ingredients. Stir gently. Makes about 1 1/2 cups (375 mL). Serves 1.

1 serving: 187 Calories; 0.1 g Total Fat (0 g Mono, 0 g Poly, 0 g Sat); 0 mg Cholesterol; 27 g Carbohydrate; trace Fibre; 0 g Protein; 13 mg Sodium

Variation: For a milder ginger flavour, omit ginger beer. Use same amount of ginger ale.

Ginger Orange Dream

A smooth blend of orange and ginger to warm the insides.

Ginger Orange Liqueur, page 138 (1 1/4 oz.)	2 1/2 tbsp.	37 mL
Orange Dream Liqueur, page 139 (3/4 oz.)	1 1/2 tbsp.	25 mL
Ice cubes	2 – 4	2 – 4
Orange slice, for garnish	1	1

Measure both liqueurs into cocktail shaker. Add ice cubes. Replace lid. Hold firmly and shake vigorously until cold. Strain through sieve into small glass. Makes about 1/3 cup (75 mL).

Garnish with orange slice. Serves 1.

1 serving: 140 Calories; 0.8 g Total Fat (0.2 g Mono, 0 g Poly, 0.5 g Sat); 3 mg Cholesterol; 13 g Carbohydrate; trace Fibre; 1 g Protein; 12 mg Sodium

Cranberry Charm

Sweet and fruity, with a licorice finish.

Cranberry cocktail	1 cup	250 mL
Frozen concentrated orange juice	1/4 cup	60 mL
Yellow-coloured, licorice-flavoured liqueur (such as Galliano), 1 oz. (see Note)	2 tbsp.	30 mL
Melon-flavoured liqueur (such as Bols), 1 oz.	2 tbsp.	30 mL
Ice cubes	4	4

Measure first 4 ingredients into cocktail shaker. Add ice cubes. Replace lid. Hold firmly and shake vigorously until cold. Strain through sieve into 2 small glasses. Makes about 1 1/2 cups (375 mL). Serves 2.

1 serving: 259 Calories; 0.3 g Total Fat (0 g Mono, 0.1 g Poly, 0.1 g Sat); 0 mg Cholesterol; 49 g Carbohydrate; trace Fibre; 1 g Protein; 6 mg Sodium

Note: If you cannot find Galliano, add several drops of yellow liquid food colouring to same amount of clear licorice-flavoured liqueur (such as Sambuca) until desired shade is reached.

Jelly Bean

Looks like grape, but tastes like licorice. A pleasant surprise!

Ice cubes	3	3
Licorice-flavoured liqueur (such as Sambuca), 3/4 oz.	1 1/2 tbsp.	25 mL
Blue-coloured, orange-flavoured liqueur (such as Blue Curaçao), 1/2 oz. (see Note)	1 tbsp.	15 mL
Grenadine syrup	1 tbsp.	15 mL
Lemon lime soft drink	3/4 cup	175 mL

Put ice cubes into medium glass. Add remaining 4 ingredients. Stir gently. Makes about 1 cup (250 mL). Serves 1.

1 serving: 250 Calories; 0.1 g Total Fat (0 g Mono, 0 g Poly, 0 g Sat); 0 mg Cholesterol; 45 g Carbohydrate; 0 g Fibre; 0 g Protein; 37 mg Sodium

Pictured on page 89.

Note: If you cannot find Blue Curaçao, add several drops of blue liquid food colouring to same amount of clear Curaçao until desired shade is reached.

Pepper Martini

A twist on the traditional martini. Warms you from the inside out.

Peppercorn Vodka, page 149 (2 oz.)	1/4 cup	60 mL
Dry vermouth (1/8 oz.)	3/4 tsp.	4 mL
Ice cubes	2 – 4	2 – 4

Lemon twist (or olive), for garnish

Measure vodka and dry vermouth into cocktail shaker. Add ice cubes. Replace lid. Hold firmly and shake vigorously until cold. Strain through sieve into martini glass (see page 8). Makes about 1/3 cup (75 mL).

Garnish with lemon twist. Serves 1.

1 serving: 140 Calories; 0 g Total Fat (0 g Mono, 0 g Poly, 0 g Sat); 0 mg Cholesterol; 0 g Carbohydrate; 0 g Fibre; 0 g Protein; 1 mg Sodium

Cocktails

Limey Coconut

Remember the old Harry Nilsson song "You put the lime in the coconut...?"
You may feel like singing it as you make this frothy, creamy drink.

Half-and-half cream (or milk)	2 tbsp.	30 mL
Coconut-flavoured rum (such as Malibu), 1/2 oz.	1 tbsp.	15 mL
White (light) rum (1/2 oz.)	1 tbsp.	15 mL
Cream of coconut	1 tbsp.	15 mL
Lime juice	1 tbsp.	15 mL
Crushed ice	1/2 cup	125 mL
Lime twist, for garnish	1	1

Measure first 5 ingredients into cocktail shaker. Add crushed ice. Replace lid. Hold firmly and shake vigorously until cold. Strain through sieve into small glass. Makes about 2/3 cup (150 mL).

Garnish with lime twist. Serves 1.

1 serving: 156 Calories; 8.4 g Total Fat (1.1 g Mono, 0.2 g Poly, 6.6 g Sat); 10 mg Cholesterol; 4 g Carbohydrate; trace Fibre; 2 g Protein; 14 mg Sodium

Ginger Fizz

Bright orange drink infused with intense ginger flavour.
Sure to add zip to your day!

Ice cubes	4	4
Pineapple juice	1/2 cup	125 mL
Apricot nectar	1/4 cup	60 mL
Ginger beer	1/4 cup	60 mL
Ginger Orange Liqueur, page 138 (1 oz.)	2 tbsp.	30 mL

Put ice cubes into large glass. Add remaining 4 ingredients. Stir gently. Makes about 1 3/4 cups (425 mL). Serves 1.

1 serving: 198 Calories; 0.2 g Total Fat (0 g Mono, 0.1 g Poly, 0 g Sat); 0 mg Cholesterol; 38 g Carbohydrate; 1 g Fibre; 1 g Protein; 8 mg Sodium

Variation: For a milder ginger flavour, omit ginger beer. Use same amount of ginger ale.

Classic Martini

Whether shaken or stirred, the proportions in these recipes can be varied to suit your personal taste: the less vermouth, the drier the drink. Crisp, cold, dry—the ultimate martini. Simple to prepare, elegant to serve.

Gin (1 1/2 oz.)	3 tbsp.	50 mL
Dry vermouth (3/4 oz.)	1 1/2 tbsp.	25 mL
Ice cubes	2 – 4	2 – 4
Pimiento-stuffed olives	2	2

Stirred Method: Measure gin and dry vermouth into 1 cup (250 mL) liquid measure. Add ice cubes. Stir until cold. Strain through sieve into martini glass (see page 8). Makes about 1/3 cup (75 mL).

Thread olives onto cocktail pick. Place in glass. Serves 1.

Shaken Method: Measure gin and dry vermouth into cocktail shaker. Add ice cubes. Replace lid. Hold firmly and shake vigorously until cold. Strain through sieve into martini glass (see page 8). Makes about 1/3 cup (75 mL).

Thread olives onto cocktail pick. Place in glass. Serves 1.

1 serving: 131 Calories; 2 g Total Fat (1.4 g Mono, 0.2 g Poly, 0.3 g Sat); 0 mg Cholesterol; 0 g Carbohydrate; 1 g Fibre; 0 g Protein; 376 mg Sodium

VODKA MARTINI: Omit gin. Use same amount of vodka.

DRY MARTINI: Measure 1/4 cup (60 mL, 2 oz.) gin and 1/2 tbsp. (7 mL, 1/4 oz.) dry vermouth into liquid measure or cocktail shaker. Add ice cubes. Stir or shake until cold. Strain through sieve into martini glass (see page 8). Garnish with olives.

Serving Suggestion: Lemon twists are an attractive alternative to the traditional olive-embellished martini. Choose a pickled onion instead and you've just made a "Gibson!"

Oogy Wawa

A booze-y, fruity drink for those hot summer days
after the yard work is done.

Pineapple juice	2 tbsp.	30 mL
Orange juice	2 tbsp.	30 mL
Apricot nectar	2 tbsp.	30 mL
Dark (navy) rum (1 oz.)	2 tbsp.	30 mL
White (light) rum (1/2 oz.)	1 tbsp.	15 mL
Lime juice	1 tbsp.	15 mL
Grenadine syrup	1/8 tsp.	0.5 mL
Bitters (such as Angostura)	3 drops	3 drops
Club soda	1/4 cup	60 mL
Crushed ice	1/4 cup	60 mL

Measure first 9 ingredients into cocktail shaker. Add crushed ice. Replace lid. Hold firmly and shake vigorously until cold. Strain through sieve into medium glass. Makes about 1 cup (250 mL). Serves 1.

1 serving: 155 Calories; 0.1 g Total Fat (0 g Mono, 0 g Poly, 0 g Sat); 0 mg Cholesterol; 14 g Carbohydrate; trace Fibre; 1 g Protein; 16 mg Sodium

Pictured on page 90.

Serving Suggestion: Dampen rim of glass with lime wedge, or dip into lime juice in saucer. Press rim into medium sweetened coconut, toasted (see Tip, page 23), in separate saucer until coated.

Paré Pointer
Say cheers in Zulu: "Oogy Wawa!" (OO-gee WAH-wah)

Morning Glory

Tart lemon and licorice are a delightful mix.

Half-and-half cream (or milk)	2 tbsp.	30 mL
Lemon juice	1 1/2 tbsp.	25 mL
Licorice-flavoured liqueur (such as Sambuca), 1/2 oz.	1 tbsp.	15 mL
Egg white (large), see Note	1	1
Ice cubes	2 – 4	2 – 4
Lemon peel spiral, for garnish	1	1

Measure first 4 ingredients into cocktail shaker. Add ice cubes. Replace lid. Hold firmly and shake vigorously until cold. Strain through sieve into small glass. Makes about 1/2 cup (125 mL).

Garnish with lemon peel spiral. Serves 1.

1 serving: 122 Calories; 3.1 g Total Fat (0.9 g Mono, 0.1 g Poly, 1.9 g Sat); 10 mg Cholesterol; 11 g Carbohydrate; trace Fibre; 4 g Protein; 68 mg Sodium

Note: Eggs used in beverages should be cold. Remove egg from refrigerator just before adding. Beverages containing uncooked egg should be served immediately.

1. Cran-Razz Soda, page 82
2. Robin's Egg, page 96
3. Jelly Bean, page 84
4. Melon Cooler, page 96

Props Courtesy Of: Mikasa Home Store

Cocktails

Blue Dazzler

Looks like a calm, clear blue ocean on a sunny day.
Light, refreshing and smooth.

Sparkling lemonade	1/2 cup	125 mL
Blue-coloured, orange-flavoured liqueur (such as Blue Curaçao), 1/2 oz. (see Note)	1 tbsp.	15 mL
Tequila (1/2 oz.)	1 tbsp.	15 mL
Scotch-based liqueur (such as Drambuie), 1/2 oz.	1 tbsp.	15 mL
Crushed ice	1/2 cup	125 mL
Lemon twist, for garnish	1	1

Measure first 4 ingredients into cocktail shaker. Add crushed ice. Replace lid. Hold firmly and shake vigorously until cold. Strain through sieve into small glass. Makes about 1 cup (250 mL).

Garnish with lemon twist. Serves 1.

1 serving: 177 Calories; 0.1 g Total Fat (0 g Mono, 0 g Poly, 0 g Sat); 0 mg Cholesterol; 22 g Carbohydrate; 0 g Fibre; 0 g Protein; 6 mg Sodium

Pictured on page 90.

Note: If you cannot find Blue Curaçao, add several drops of blue liquid food colouring to same amount of clear Curaçao until desired shade is reached.

1. Tropical Breeze, page 75
2. Sunburn, page 95
3. Blue Dazzler, above
4. Oogy Wawa, page 87

Props Courtesy Of: Pier 1 Imports
The Bay

Orange Almond Cocktail

*Red grenadine settles to the bottom of the glass for
an attractive, vibrant presentation. It's delicious, too.*

Orange juice	1 cup	250 mL
Vodka (2 oz.)	1/4 cup	60 mL
Almond-flavoured liqueur (such as Amaretto), 1 oz.	2 tbsp.	30 mL
Ice cubes	4	4
Crushed ice	1/4 cup	60 mL
Grenadine syrup	1/4 tsp.	1 mL

Measure orange juice, vodka and liqueur into cocktail shaker. Add ice
cubes. Replace lid. Hold firmly and shake vigorously until cold. Strain
through sieve into 2 cup (500 mL) liquid measure. Makes about 1 1/3 cups
(325 mL).

Spoon crushed ice into 2 small glasses. Pour orange juice mixture over top.
Drizzle each with grenadine. Do not stir. Serves 2.

*1 serving: 193 Calories; 0.3 g Total Fat (0.1 g Mono, 0.1 g Poly, 0 g Sat); 0 mg Cholesterol;
21 g Carbohydrate; trace Fibre; 1 g Protein; 3 mg Sodium*

Pictured on front cover.

Serving Suggestion: Serve this drink in martini glasses (see page 8) to
show off its colour.

Paré Pointer
Say cheers in Italian: "Alla salute!" (AH-lah sal-OO-tay)

Cocktails

Pearl Drop

Creamy white chocolate flavour with a surprise at the bottom of the glass!

Milk chocolate kiss	1	1
Half-and-half cream (or milk)	2 tbsp.	30 mL
Vodka (1 oz.)	2 tbsp.	30 mL
Chocolate-flavoured liqueur (such as Crème de cacao), 1/4 oz.	1/2 tbsp.	7 mL
Irish cream liqueur (such as Baileys), 1/4 oz.	1/2 tbsp.	7 mL
Ice cubes	2 – 4	2 – 4

Place chocolate kiss in bottom of small glass.

Measure next 4 ingredients into cocktail shaker. Add ice cubes. Replace lid. Hold firmly and shake vigorously until cold. Strain through sieve into prepared glass. Makes about 1/3 cup (75 mL). Serves 1.

1 serving: 173 Calories; 6.8 g Total Fat (2 g Mono, 0.3 g Poly, 4.2 g Sat); 13 mg Cholesterol; 7 g Carbohydrate; trace Fibre; 2 g Protein; 31 mg Sodium

Serving Suggestion: This is a fun drink to serve in a martini glass (see page 8).

Curried Tomato Juice

A good aperitif for a summer barbecue. Mild curry flavour in a creamy, tangy tomato drink.

Tomato juice	1 cup	250 mL
Buttermilk	1/4 cup	60 mL
Gin (1 oz.), optional	2 tbsp.	30 mL
Plain yogurt	1 tbsp.	15 mL
Curry paste	1/4 tsp.	1 mL
Ice cubes	4	4

Measure first 5 ingredients into cocktail shaker. Add ice cubes. Replace lid. Hold firmly and shake vigorously until creamy and cold. Strain through sieve into 2 small glasses. Makes about 1 1/2 cups (375 mL). Serves 2.

1 serving (with alcohol): 73 Calories; 0.5 g Total Fat (0.1 g Mono, 0.1 g Poly, 0.3 g Sat); 2 mg Cholesterol; 8 g Carbohydrate; 1 g Fibre; 3 g Protein; 509 mg Sodium

Spiced Berry

Ruby red with subtle spice and full berry flavours.

Cranberry cocktail	3/4 cup	175 mL
Spiced rum (1 1/2 oz.)	3 tbsp.	50 mL
Raspberry-flavoured liqueur (such as Chambord), 3/4 oz.	1 1/2 tbsp.	25 mL
Ice cubes	4	4

Measure first 3 ingredients into cocktail shaker. Add ice cubes. Replace lid. Hold firmly and shake vigorously until cold. Strain through sieve into 2 small glasses. Makes about 1 1/4 cups (300 mL). Serves 2.

1 serving: 114 Calories; 0.1 g Total Fat (0 g Mono, 0 g Poly, 0 g Sat); 0 mg Cholesterol; 14 g Carbohydrate; 0 g Fibre; 0 g Protein; 2 mg Sodium

Serving Suggestion: Combine 3 tbsp. (50 mL) granulated sugar and 1 tsp. (5 mL) ground cinnamon in saucer. Dip rims of 2 martini glasses (see page 8) into cranberry cocktail in separate saucer. Press into sugar mixture until coated. Pour cocktail mixture into glasses.

Sham Champagne

This recipe can be easily increased to make a large quantity. The sugar cube produces a steady supply of small bubbles—just like the real thing.

White grape juice	1/2 cup	125 mL
Club soda	1/2 cup	125 mL
Sugar cube (optional)	1	1

Measure grape juice and club soda into champagne flute (see page 8). Stir gently.

Drop sugar cube into grape juice mixture. Makes 1 cup (250 mL). Serve immediately. Serves 1.

1 serving: 82 Calories; 0.1 g Total Fat (0 g Mono, 0 g Poly, 0 g Sat); 0 mg Cholesterol; 20 g Carbohydrate; trace Fibre; 1 g Protein; 31 mg Sodium

Cocktails

Sunburn

Attractive tangerine-red colour with a pleasing fruity flavour.

Ice cubes	4	4
Mango tangerine cocktail (such as Sunrype)	2/3 cup	150 mL
Pineapple juice	1/3 cup	75 mL
Dark (navy) rum (3/4 oz.)	1 1/2 tbsp.	25 mL
Grenadine syrup	1 tbsp.	15 mL
Almond-flavoured liqueur (such as Amaretto), 1/4 oz.	1/2 tbsp.	7 mL
Peach-flavoured liqueur (such as Southern Comfort), 1/4 oz.	1/2 tbsp.	7 mL

Put ice cubes into large glass. Add remaining 6 ingredients. Stir. Makes about 1 1/4 cups (300 mL). Serves 1.

1 serving: 297 Calories; 0.5 g Total Fat (0.1 g Mono, 0.1 g Poly, 0.1 g Sat); 0 mg Cholesterol; 54 g Carbohydrate; trace Fibre; 0 g Protein; 25 mg Sodium

Pictured on page 90.

Tropical Sunrise

Luscious, citrus-filled beverage. Pure ambrosia!

Pineapple juice	1 cup	250 mL
Frozen concentrated orange juice	1/4 cup	60 mL
Coconut milk	1/4 cup	60 mL
Crushed ice	3 tbsp.	50 mL
Lime juice	1 tbsp.	15 mL

Process all 5 ingredients in blender until smooth. Makes about 1 3/4 cups (425 mL). Pour into 2 medium glasses. Serves 2.

1 serving: 195 Calories; 6.6 g Total Fat (0.3 g Mono, 0.1 g Poly, 5.7 g Sat); 0 mg Cholesterol; 34 g Carbohydrate; trace Fibre; 2 g Protein; 6 mg Sodium

VODKA SUNRISE: Add 1/4 cup (60 mL, 2 oz.) vodka or white (light) rum to blender with all 5 ingredients. Process until smooth. Makes about 2 cups (500 mL).

Robin's Egg

The robin's egg blue colour catches your eye. The combination of orange and chocolate satisfies your taste buds.

Ice cubes	4	4
Blue-coloured, orange-flavoured liqueur (such as Blue Curaçao), 3/4 oz. (see Note)	1 1/2 tbsp.	25 mL
White chocolate-flavoured liqueur (such as Godet), 1/2 oz.	1 tbsp.	15 mL
Milk	1/2 cup	125 mL

Put ice cubes into medium glass. Add both liqueurs and milk. Stir. Makes about 2/3 cup (150 mL). Serves 1.

1 serving: 195 Calories; 3.9 g Total Fat (1.1 g Mono, 0.2 g Poly, 2.4 g Sat); 8 mg Cholesterol; 22 g Carbohydrate; 0 g Fibre; 5 g Protein; 81 mg Sodium

Pictured on page 89.

Note: If you cannot find Blue Curaçao, add several drops of blue liquid food colouring to same amount of clear Curaçao until desired shade is reached.

Melon Cooler

Sweet, sparkling cooler for a hot summer's day.

Melon-flavoured liqueur (such as Bols), 1/2 oz.	1 tbsp.	15 mL
Sparkling sweet wine (such as Asti Spumante), 4 oz.	1/2 cup	125 mL

Measure liqueur into small glass. Add sparkling wine. Stir gently. Makes about 1/2 cup (125 mL). Serves 1.

1 serving: 117 Calories; 0 g Total Fat (0 g Mono, 0 g Poly, 0 g Sat); 0 mg Cholesterol; 1 g Carbohydrate; 0 g Fibre; 0 g Protein; 6 mg Sodium

Pictured on page 89.

Serving Suggestion: Serve this cooler in a cocktail glass or champagne flute (see page 8) for an attractive presentation.

Raspberry Spritzer

*Sweet ginger ale releases the fresh raspberry flavour
in this brilliant red drink. Pretty and festive.*

Package of frozen raspberries in syrup, thawed	15 oz.	425 g
Ginger ale	3 cups	750 mL

Press raspberries through sieve into small bowl or 2 cup (500 mL) liquid measure. Discard seeds. Makes about 1 1/4 cups (300 mL) juice. Measure 3 tbsp. (50 mL) juice into each of 6 small glasses.

Add 1/2 cup (125 mL) ginger ale to each. Stir gently. Serves 6.

1 serving: 117 Calories; 0.1 g Total Fat (0 g Mono, 0.1 g Poly, 0 g Sat); 0 mg Cholesterol; 30 g Carbohydrate; 3 g Fibre; 1 g Protein; 10 mg Sodium

Pictured on front cover.

Pineapple Alaska

Light yellow foam tops this fluffy pineapple treat.

Crushed ice	2 cups	500 mL
Can of crushed pineapple (with juice)	14 oz.	398 mL
Pineapple juice	1/2 cup	125 mL
Brown sugar, packed	1 1/2 tbsp.	25 mL
Egg white (large), see Note	1	1

Process all 5 ingredients in blender until cream-coloured and foamy. Makes about 6 2/3 cups (1.65 L). Pour into 6 medium glasses. Let stand for 1 minute. Foam will rise to top. Serves 6.

1 serving: 70 Calories; 0.1 g Total Fat (0 g Mono, 0 g Poly, 0 g Sat); 0 mg Cholesterol; 18 g Carbohydrate; 1 g Fibre; 1 g Protein; 11 mg Sodium

Note: Eggs used in beverages should be cold. Remove egg from refrigerator just before adding. Beverages containing uncooked egg should be served immediately.

PINEAPPLE RUM ALASKA: Add 6 tbsp. (100 mL, 3 oz.) white (light) rum to ingredients in blender before processing.

Orange Apricot Delight

*Subtle hint of licorice makes this smooth,
fruity beverage delightfully different.*

Orange juice	1/2 cup	125 mL
Apricot brandy (1 1/2 oz.)	3 tbsp.	50 mL
Vodka (1 oz.)	2 tbsp.	30 mL
Yellow-coloured, licorice-flavoured liqueur (such as Galliano), 1/2 oz. (see Note)	1 tbsp.	15 mL
Ginger ale	1/2 cup	125 mL
Ice		

Combine first 4 ingredients in 2 cup (500 mL) liquid measure. Add ginger ale. Stir gently. Makes about 1 1/2 cups (375 mL). Pour over ice in 2 small glasses. Serves 2.

1 serving: 164 Calories; 0.2 g Total Fat (0 g Mono, 0 g Poly, 0 g Sat); 0 mg Cholesterol; 16 g Carbohydrate; trace Fibre; 0 g Protein; 6 mg Sodium

Note: If you cannot find Galliano, add several drops of yellow liquid food colouring to same amount of clear licorice-flavoured liqueur (such as Sambuca) until desired shade is reached.

Strawberry Blonde

Sparkling apple cider is a perfect partner to Madeira—a sweet, fortified wine that gives this drink its unusual colour and taste.

Ice cubes	4 – 5	4 – 5
Sparkling apple cider	3/4 cup	175 mL
Madeira wine (1 1/2 oz.)	3 tbsp.	50 mL
Grenadine syrup	1/8 tsp.	0.5 mL
Fresh strawberry, for garnish	1	1

Put ice cubes into medium glass. Add apple cider, wine and grenadine. Stir gently. Makes about 1 cup (250 mL).

Garnish with strawberry. Serves 1.

1 serving: 128 Calories; 0.2 g Total Fat (0 g Mono, 0.1 g Poly, 0 g Sat); 0 mg Cholesterol; 25 g Carbohydrate; trace Fibre; 0 g Protein; 9 mg Sodium

Cocktails

Misty Evening

Soothing beverage with a lemon mist.

Whole cloves	3	3
Lemon slice (1/2 inch, 12 mm, thick)	1	1
Cinnamon stick (4 inches, 10 cm)	1	1
Boiling water	2/3 cup	150 mL
Canadian whisky (rye), 1 oz.	2 tbsp.	30 mL
Liquid honey	1 tsp.	5 mL

Place first 3 ingredients in small mug.

Add boiling water, whisky and honey. Stir, using cinnamon stick. Let stand for 2 to 3 minutes. Remove and discard cloves, lemon slice and cinnamon stick. Makes about 1 cup (250 mL). Serves 1.

1 serving: 87 Calories; 0 g Total Fat (0 g Mono, 0 g Poly, 0 g Sat); 0 mg Cholesterol; 6 g Carbohydrate; 0 g Fibre; 0 g Protein; 1 mg Sodium

Pictured on page 107.

Serving Suggestion: Add a fresh cinnamon stick wrapped with a spiral of lemon zest to mug for garnish.

Nutty Irish

Nutty flavour with a creamy texture. A comforting late-night drink.

Milk	1 cup	250 mL
Hazelnut-flavoured liqueur (such as Frangelico), 1/2 oz.	1 tbsp.	15 mL
Irish cream liqueur (such as Baileys), 1/2 oz.	1 tbsp.	15 mL

Heat and stir milk in small heavy saucepan on medium until bubbles form around edge. Remove from heat.

Add both liqueurs. Stir. Makes about 1 cup (250 mL). Pour into small mug. Serves 1.

1 serving: 214 Calories; 5.3 g Total Fat (1.5 g Mono, 0.2 g Poly, 3.2 g Sat); 13 mg Cholesterol; 21 g Carbohydrate; 0 g Fibre; 9 g Protein; 145 mg Sodium

Dutch Eggnog

Creamy yellow with a sprinkle of spice.

Milk	3/4 cup	175 mL
Apricot brandy (1/2 oz.)	1 tbsp.	15 mL
Apricot nectar	1 tbsp.	15 mL
Eggnog-flavoured liqueur (such as Advocaat), 1 oz.	2 tbsp.	30 mL
Ground nutmeg, sprinkle		

Heat and stir milk, brandy and apricot nectar in small heavy saucepan on medium until bubbles form around edge. Remove from heat.

Add liqueur. Stir. Makes about 1 cup (250 mL). Pour into small mug. Sprinkle with nutmeg. Serves 1.

1 serving: 188 Calories; 2.1 g Total Fat (0.6 g Mono, 0.1 g Poly, 1.3 g Sat); 8 mg Cholesterol; 12 g Carbohydrate; trace Fibre; 6 g Protein; 98 mg Sodium

Serving Suggestion: Add extra nutmeg for a more traditional eggnog.

Snow-Capped Mountain

This drink will remind you of a purple mountain with a snow-covered peak.

Milk	3/4 cup	175 mL
Raspberry-flavoured liqueur (such as Chambord), 3/4 oz.	1 1/2 tbsp.	25 mL
Vodka (1/2 oz.)	1 tbsp.	15 mL
Whipped cream (or frozen whipped topping, thawed)	2 tbsp.	30 mL

Heat and stir milk in small heavy saucepan on medium until bubbles form around edge. Remove from heat.

Add liqueur and vodka. Stir. Makes about 1 cup (250 mL). Pour into small glass mug.

Top with whipped cream. Serves 1.

1 serving: 209 Calories; 6.9 g Total Fat (2 g Mono, 0.2 g Poly, 4.3 g Sat); 25 mg Cholesterol; 10 g Carbohydrate; 0 g Fibre; 7 g Protein; 103 mg Sodium

Toasted Almond

Fragrant almond and coffee aromas emanate from this soothing, warm milk.

Milk	1 1/2 cups	375 mL
Almond-flavoured liqueur (such as Amaretto), 1 oz.	2 tbsp.	30 mL
Coffee-flavoured liqueur (such as Kahlúa), 1 oz.	2 tbsp.	30 mL
Whipped cream (or frozen whipped topping, thawed), for garnish	2 tbsp.	30 mL
Finely chopped almonds, toasted (see Tip, page 23), for garnish	1 tbsp.	15 mL

Heat and stir milk in small heavy saucepan on medium until bubbles form around edge. Remove from heat.

Add both liqueurs. Stir. Makes about 1 1/2 cups (375 mL). Pour into 2 small mugs.

Top each with whipped cream and almonds. Serves 2.

1 serving: 199 Calories; 2.2 g Total Fat (0.6 g Mono, 0.1 g Poly, 1.3 g Sat); 8 mg Cholesterol; 22 g Carbohydrate; 0 g Fibre; 6 g Protein; 99 mg Sodium

Applecot Cider

Sweet apple cider mingled with tangy apricot and ginger.

Package of apple cider mix (such as Lynch)	3/4 oz.	23 g
Apricot brandy (1/2 oz.)	1 tbsp.	15 mL
Ginger Orange Liqueur, page 138 (or peach-flavoured liqueur, such as peach schnapps), 1/2 oz.	1 tbsp.	15 mL

Prepare apple cider mix in small mug according to package directions.

Add brandy and liqueur. Stir. Makes about 1 cup (250 mL). Serves 1.

1 serving: 188 Calories; 0.3 g Total Fat (0 g Mono, 0.1 g Poly, 0.1 g Sat); 0 mg Cholesterol; 33 g Carbohydrate; trace Fibre; 0 g Protein; 8 mg Sodium

Maple Toddy

Apple and vanilla flavours with the sweetness of maple syrup.

Apple cider (or apple juice)	4 cups	1 L
Maple (or maple-flavoured) syrup	3 tbsp.	50 mL
Vanilla bean, split	1	1
Cinnamon stick (4 inches, 10 cm)	1	1
Whole allspice	10	10
Brandy (2 1/2 oz.), optional	1/3 cup	75 mL

Combine first 5 ingredients in medium saucepan. Bring to a boil on medium. Reduce heat to medium-low. Simmer, uncovered, for about 25 minutes until fragrant. Remove from heat. Strain through sieve into 4 cup (1 L) liquid measure. Discard solids.

Add brandy. Stir. Makes about 3 1/3 cups (825 mL). Pour into 4 small mugs. Serves 4.

1 serving: 162 Calories; 0.3 g Total Fat (0 g Mono, 0.1 g Poly, 0.1 g Sat); 0 mg Cholesterol; 41 g Carbohydrate; trace Fibre; 0 g Protein; 9 mg Sodium

Pictured on page 107.

Serving Suggestion: Add a fresh cinnamon stick for garnish, or serve with maple-flavoured chocolates.

Last Call

Sweet apple cider with a black raspberry finish. Delicious!

Package of apple cider mix (such as Lynch)	3/4 oz.	23 g
Boiling water	1 cup	250 mL
Raspberry-flavoured liqueur (such as Chambord), 1 oz.	2 tbsp.	30 mL
Cinnamon stick (4 inches, 10 cm)	1	1

Combine apple cider mix and boiling water in large mug.

Add liqueur. Stir. Makes about 1 cup (250 mL). Add cinnamon stick. Serves 1.

1 serving: 242 Calories; 0.4 g Total Fat (0 g Mono, 0.1 g Poly, 0.1 g Sat); 0 mg Cholesterol; 47 g Carbohydrate; trace Fibre; 0 g Protein; 11 mg Sodium

Nightcaps

Sweet Dreams

Two-layered dessert in a glass. Well worth the extra effort.
The foamy egg layer makes this drink a decadent dream.

Chocolate milk	2 1/2 cups	625 mL
Almond-flavoured liqueur (such as Amaretto), 4 oz.	1/2 cup	125 mL
ORANGE SABAYON		
Egg yolks (large)	2	2
Granulated sugar	2 1/2 tbsp.	37 mL
Orange juice	2 tbsp.	30 mL

Heat and stir chocolate milk in heavy medium saucepan on medium until bubbles form around edge. Remove from heat.

Add liqueur. Stir. Cover to keep warm. Makes about 3 cups (750 mL).

Orange Sabayon: Beat egg yolks and sugar on medium in small bowl over saucepan of simmering water for about 1 minute until combined. Add orange juice. Beat for about 5 minutes until foamy and thickened. Makes about 1 1/4 cups (300 mL) sabayon.

Pour about 3/4 cup (175 mL) chocolate milk mixture into each of 4 large mugs. Top each with about 1/3 cup (75 mL) sabayon. Serves 4.

1 serving: 314 Calories; 6 g Total Fat (2 g Mono, 0.5 g Poly, 2.9 g Sat); 119 mg Cholesterol; 41 g Carbohydrate; 1 g Fibre; 7 g Protein; 105 mg Sodium

Pictured on page 18 and on back cover.

Variation (without alcohol): Omit liqueur. Use same amount of almond-flavoured syrup (such as Torani's).

Serving Suggestion: Garnish with chocolate curls. To make curls, peel room temperature chocolate with vegetable peeler.

Sunset Tea

A mellow blend of orange and almond flavours in a dusk-red tea.
Fill your cup and enjoy the evening twilight.

Boiling water	2 cups	500 mL
Orange and peach-flavoured tea bags (such as Tetley)	2	2
Cognac (or brandy), 1/2 oz.	1 tbsp.	15 mL
Almond-flavoured liqueur (such as Amaretto), 1/2 oz.	1 tbsp.	15 mL
Orange-flavoured liqueur (such as Grand Marnier), 1 oz.	2 tbsp.	30 mL
Lemon juice	2 tsp.	10 mL

Pour boiling water into teapot. Add tea bags. Cover. Let steep for 5 minutes. Squeeze and discard tea bags.

Add remaining 4 ingredients. Stir. Makes about 2 1/2 cups (625 mL). Pour into 2 large mugs. Serves 2.

1 serving: 84 Calories; 0 g Total Fat (0 g Mono, 0 g Poly, 0 g Sat); 0 mg Cholesterol; 4 g Carbohydrate; 0 g Fibre; 0 g Protein; 3 mg Sodium

Serving Suggestion: Add a citrus knot to each cup of tea for extra zest. To make knots, choose firm, smooth-skinned orange, lemon or lime. Wash and dry fruit. Remove 4 inch (10 cm) thin strip of peel from fruit, using citrus stripper. Tie peel in a knot and drop into tea.

Minty Thaw

Tastes like a peppermint patty!

Chocolate milk	2 cups	500 mL
Mint-flavoured liqueur (such as peppermint schnapps), 2 oz.	1/4 cup	60 mL
Whipped cream (or frozen whipped topping, thawed), optional	2 tbsp.	30 mL

(continued on next page)

Heat and stir chocolate milk in small heavy saucepan on medium until bubbles form around edge. Remove from heat.

Add liqueur. Stir. Makes about 2 1/2 cups (625 mL). Pour into 2 large mugs.

Top each with whipped cream. Serves 2.

1 serving: 322 Calories; 5.4 g Total Fat (1.6 g Mono, 0.3 g Poly, 3.3 g Sat); 18 mg Cholesterol; 42 g Carbohydrate; 2 g Fibre; 8 g Protein; 161 mg Sodium

Pictured on page 107.

Serving Suggestion: Sprinkle crushed mint candies over whipped cream for colour, and add a candy cane or peppermint stick for stirring.

White Hot Chocolate

Oh, so sweet and chocolaty! A dessert you can drink.

Milk	1 cup	250 mL
White chocolate bar, chopped (about 1/2 cup, 125 mL)	3 1/2 oz.	100 g
Vanilla	1/4 tsp.	1 mL
Whipped cream (or frozen whipped topping, thawed)	1/4 cup	60 mL

Heat and stir milk in small heavy saucepan on medium until bubbles form around edge. Remove from heat.

Add chocolate bar pieces and vanilla. Stir until chocolate is melted and mixture is smooth. Makes about 1 1/3 cups (325 mL). Pour into 2 small mugs.

Top each with whipped cream. Serves 2.

1 serving: 370 Calories; 21.7 g Total Fat (6.7 g Mono, 0.6 g Poly, 12.9 g Sat); 35 mg Cholesterol; 37 g Carbohydrate; 0 g Fibre; 8 g Protein; 115 mg Sodium

Serving Suggestion: Use espresso cups for this decadent dessert beverage—a little goes a long way! Serves 4.

After-Dinner Mint

Minted chocolate with an eggnog flavour and a chocolate stir stick.

Chocolate milk	3/4 cup	175 mL
Mint-flavoured liqueur (such as Crème de menthe), 1/4 oz.	1/2 tbsp.	7 mL
Chocolate-flavoured liqueur (such as Crème de cacao), 1/2 oz.	1 tbsp.	15 mL
Eggnog-flavoured liqueur (such as Advocaat), 1/2 oz. (optional)	1 tbsp.	15 mL
Chocolate stick with mint filling (such as Ovation), for garnish	1	1

Heat and stir chocolate milk in small heavy saucepan on medium until bubbles form around edge. Remove from heat.

Add all 3 liqueurs. Stir. Makes about 1 cup (250 mL). Pour into large mug.

Garnish with chocolate stick. Serves 1.

1 serving: 225 Calories; 6.5 g Total Fat (1.9 g Mono, 0.3 g Poly, 4 g Sat); 16 mg Cholesterol; 28 g Carbohydrate; 1 g Fibre; 7 g Protein; 135 mg Sodium

1. Minty Thaw, page 104
2. Misty Evening, page 99
3. Maple Toddy, page 102

Props Courtesy Of: Wal-Mart Canada Inc.

Vanilla Milk

Can't sleep? This beats counting sheep to help you relax.

Milk	2 cups	500 mL
White corn syrup	3 tbsp.	50 mL
Clear vanilla	2 tsp.	10 mL

Heat and stir all 3 ingredients in small heavy saucepan on medium until bubbles form around edge. Makes about 2 cups (500 mL). Pour into 2 small mugs. Serves 2.

1 serving: 217 Calories; 2.7 g Total Fat (0.8 g Mono, 0.1 g Poly, 1.7 g Sat); 10 mg Cholesterol; 38 g Carbohydrate; 0 g Fibre; 8 g Protein; 151 mg Sodium

Variation: Omit corn syrup and vanilla. Use 3 tbsp. (50 mL) vanilla-flavoured syrup (such as Torani's).

VANILLA MALTED MILK: Add 3 tbsp. (50 mL) malt drink mix (such as Ovaltine) to milk mixture before heating.

VANILLA HAZELNUT MILK: Add 2 tbsp. (30 mL, 1 oz.) hazelnut-flavoured liqueur (such as Frangelico) to each mug.

1. Cran-Almond Delight, page 78
2. South Seas Sangria, page 113
3. Granny Smith, page 80
4. Berry Citrus Freeze, page 60

Props Courtesy Of: Canhome Global
Pier 1 Imports
Winners Stores

Apple Ginger Punch

Sparkling, tart apple flavour goes well with ginger. So delicious!

Tart medium cooking apples (such as Granny Smith), peeled and core removed, diced	4	4
Water	1 cup	250 mL
Brown sugar, packed	1/4 cup	60 mL
Finely grated, peeled gingerroot	2 tsp.	10 mL
Bottles of sparkling apple cider (with alcohol), 12 oz. (341 mL) each	4	4
Ginger ale	3 cups	750 mL
Ice cubes	12	12
Thin slices of apple (with peel), core removed, for garnish	12 – 16	12 – 16

Heat and stir first 4 ingredients in large saucepan on medium until mixture just starts to boil. Reduce heat to medium-low. Cover. Simmer for 10 to 15 minutes, stirring occasionally, until apple is softened. Remove from heat. Cool. Transfer to blender. Process until smooth. Transfer to small punch bowl. Cover. Chill for at least 4 hours until cold.

Just before serving, add apple cider and ginger ale. Stir gently. Add ice cubes and apple slices. Makes about 16 cups (4 L). Serves 14.

1 serving: 104 Calories; 0.1 g Total Fat (0 g Mono, 0 g Poly, 0 g Sat); 0 mg Cholesterol; 20 g Carbohydrate; 1 g Fibre; 0 g Protein; 14 mg Sodium

Variation (without alcohol): Omit sparkling apple cider (with alcohol). Use same amount of alcohol-free sparkling apple cider.

Fizzy Lemon Refresher

*Tart, but not sour, with a sweet, fizzy finish. You'll want
to pour this refreshing drink over plenty of ice.*

Boiling water	3 cups	750 mL
Medium lemons, sliced	3	3
Diced, peeled gingerroot	1 tbsp.	15 mL
Granulated sugar	1 cup	250 mL
Lemon juice	1/2 cup	125 mL
Club soda	4 cups	1 L
Ice cubes		

Pour boiling water into large heatproof bowl. Add lemon slices and ginger. Cover. Let stand at room temperature for at least 12 hours. Strain lemon mixture through sieve into medium saucepan. Discard solids.

Add sugar. Heat and stir on medium-high until boiling. Reduce heat to medium. Boil, uncovered, for 15 to 20 minutes, stirring occasionally, until reduced by half and slightly thickened. Remove from heat. Let stand until cooled completely.

Add lemon juice. Stir. Pour into pitcher. Cover. Chill for at least 4 hours until cold.

Just before serving, add club soda. Stir gently. Makes about 5 1/2 cups (1.4 L).

Pour over ice cubes in 6 medium glasses. Serves 6.

1 serving: 143 Calories; 0 g Total Fat (0 g Mono, 0 g Poly, 0 g Sat); 0 mg Cholesterol; 37 g Carbohydrate; trace Fibre; 0 g Protein; 37 mg Sodium

Paré Pointer

Say cheers in Maori: "Kia Ora!" (KEE-ah Or-AH)

Sangria

Full-bodied flavour, lightened with soda.
Fruit slices add a pretty contrast to the wine's deep red colour.

Brandy (8 oz.)	1 cup	250 mL
Granulated sugar	2/3 cup	150 mL
Medium oranges, sliced	2	2
Medium lemons, sliced	2	2
Medium limes, sliced	2	2
Bottles of dry red (or alcohol-free) wine (26 oz., 750 mL, each)	2	2
Club soda	4 cups	1 L
Ice cubes	24	24

Measure brandy and sugar into small punch bowl. Stir until sugar is dissolved. Add orange, lemon and lime slices. Stir. Cover. Let stand for 1 1/2 hours.

Add wine. Stir. Chill for at least 4 hours until cold.

Just before serving, remove citrus slices using slotted spoon, leaving 6 to 8 slices in bowl for garnish. Add club soda. Stir gently. Add ice cubes. Makes 14 cups (3.5 L). Serves 25.

1 serving: 95 Calories; 0 g Total Fat (0 g Mono, 0 g Poly, 0 g Sat); 0 mg Cholesterol; 9 g Carbohydrate; trace Fibre; 0 g Protein; 12 mg Sodium

Pictured on page 125.

South Seas Sangria

This cool wine and fruit punch has a tropical flair
and is not too sweet. Good for sipping.

Can of sliced peaches in pear juice	14 oz.	398 mL
Dry white (or alcohol-free) wine (26 oz.)	3 cups	750 mL
Pear juice (such as Ceres)	1/2 cup	125 mL
Blue-coloured, orange-flavoured liqueur (such as Blue Curaçao), 2 oz. (see Note)	1/4 cup	60 mL
Can of club soda	12 1/2 oz.	355 mL

Drain peaches, reserving juice. Chop peaches. Transfer peaches and reserved juice to pitcher.

Add wine, pear juice and liqueur. Cover. Chill for at least 4 hours until cold.

Just before serving, add club soda. Stir gently. Makes about 7 1/2 cups (1.9 L). Pour into 12 chilled small glasses. Serves 12.

1 serving: 84 Calories; 0 g Total Fat (0 g Mono, 0 g Poly, 0 g Sat); 0 mg Cholesterol; 9 g Carbohydrate; trace Fibre; 0 g Protein; 12 mg Sodium

Pictured on page 108.

Note: If you cannot find Blue Curaçao, add several drops of blue liquid food colouring to same amount of clear Curaçao until desired shade is reached.

Paré Pointer
Say cheers in Polish: "Na Zdrowoie!" (NAH zdrav-EE)

Pineapple Citrus Punch

Tangy fruit blend in a beautiful amber-coloured punch. Refreshing, flavourful and without alcohol. Add an ice ring for a decorative flair.

Pineapple juice	4 cups	1 L
Orange juice	2 cups	500 mL
Ruby red grapefruit juice	2 cups	500 mL
Lemon juice	1/4 cup	60 mL
Large oranges, peeled and sectioned, membranes and seeds discarded, cut bite size	2	2
Large pink grapefruit, peeled and sectioned, membranes and seeds discarded, cut bite size	1	1
Lemon lime soft drink	4 cups	1 L

Combine first 6 ingredients in small punch bowl. Chill for at least 4 hours until cold.

Just before serving, add lemon lime soft drink. Stir gently. Makes about 14 1/2 cups (3.6 L). Serves 25.

1 serving: 69 Calories; 0.1 g Total Fat (0 g Mono, 0 g Poly, 0 g Sat); 0 mg Cholesterol; 17 g Carbohydrate; trace Fibre; 1 g Protein; 6 mg Sodium

ICE RING: Put crushed ice into bottom of 12 cup (3 L) bundt pan. Arrange various fruit pieces in and on top of ice. Freeze for 1 hour. Pour 2 cups (500 mL) punch or fruit juice over top of fruit. (Do not use alcohol in ice ring because alcohol will not freeze.) Freeze for 8 hours or overnight. Run warm water over underside of bundt pan. Carefully remove ice ring. Gently place in punch.

Variation: To keep ice ring from thawing too quickly, omit punch or fruit juice. Use clear sugar-free soft drink, such as lemon lime or ginger ale, to pour over top of fruit.

Rhubarb Punch

Tangy and sweet—very refreshing. Make the juice
the day before for easy assembly just before guests arrive.

RHUBARB JUICE

Package of frozen (or fresh, chopped) rhubarb, thawed	2 1/4 lbs.	1 kg
Whole cloves	4	4
Water	1 cup	250 mL
Granulated sugar	1/4 cup	60 mL
Ginger ale	3 cups	750 mL
Sliced fresh strawberries	1 cup	250 mL
Ice cubes	12	12

Rhubarb Juice: Combine rhubarb, cloves and water in large saucepan. Bring to a boil on high. Reduce heat to medium-low. Cover. Simmer for about 25 minutes, stirring occasionally, until rhubarb is softened. Remove from heat. Strain through sieve into medium bowl. Press gently with back of spoon to extract juice. Discard solids.

Add sugar. Stir until sugar is dissolved. Let stand for 5 minutes. Cover. Chill for at least 4 hours until cold. Makes about 3 cups (750 mL) juice.

Pour juice into small punch bowl. Add ginger ale. Stir gently. Add strawberries and ice cubes. Makes about 8 cups (2 L). Serves 14.

1 serving: 52 Calories; 0.1 g Total Fat (0 g Mono, 0 g Poly, 0 g Sat); 0 mg Cholesterol; 13 g Carbohydrate; 1 g Fibre; 0 g Protein; 5 mg Sodium

Pictured on page 125.

Paré Pointer
Say cheers in Portuguese: Saude! (sah-OOD)

Soda-licious Punch

Peachy-pink with pretty strawberry ice cubes. Subtly sweet.

Apple juice	2 cups	500 mL
Fresh (or frozen) whole strawberries, sliced	1 cup	250 mL
Blush wine (such as Zinfandel), 26 oz.	3 cups	750 mL
Apple juice	1/2 cup	125 mL
Brandy (4 oz.)	1/2 cup	125 mL
Ginger ale	2 cups	500 mL
Club soda	2 cups	500 mL

Pour first amount of apple juice into ice cube trays for a total of about 20 cubes. Add 2 strawberry slices to each cube. Freeze for at least 4 hours until firm.

Combine wine, second amount of apple juice and brandy in small punch bowl. Add ginger ale and club soda. Stir gently. Add strawberry ice cubes. Makes about 11 cups (2.75 L). Serves 20.

1 serving: 66 Calories; 0.1 g Total Fat (0 g Mono, 0 g Poly, 0 g Sat); 0 mg Cholesterol; 7 g Carbohydrate; trace Fibre; 0 g Protein; 10 mg Sodium

Apricot Orange Punch

Easy to make, this brightly coloured punch is perfect for a party.

Cans of mandarin orange segments (with juice), 10 oz. (284 mL) each	3	3
Apricot nectar	2 cups	500 mL
Orange juice	2 cups	500 mL
Yellow-coloured lemon lime soft drink (such as Mountain Dew)	2 1/2 cups	625 mL
Ice cubes (or Ice Ring, page 114)	12	12

Combine first 3 ingredients in small punch bowl. Add lemon lime soft drink. Stir gently. Add ice cubes. Makes about 11 cups (2.75 L). Serves 20.

1 serving: 56 Calories; 0.1 g Total Fat (0 g Mono, 0 g Poly, 0 g Sat); 0 mg Cholesterol; 14 g Carbohydrate; trace Fibre; 1 g Protein; 7 mg Sodium

Cherry Lemon Sipper

Pretty, light, purple sparkling punch with a delicate dash of lemon.

Can of frozen concentrated lemonade, partially thawed	12 1/2 oz.	355 mL
Club soda	4 cups	1 L
Ginger ale	4 cups	1 L
Cherry brandy (3 oz.)	6 tbsp.	100 mL
Can of pitted Bing cherries, drained	14 oz.	398 mL

Measure first 3 ingredients into small punch bowl. Stir gently until concentrated lemonade is dissolved.

Add brandy and cherries. Stir. Makes about 11 cups (2.75 L). Serves 20.

1 serving: 77 Calories; 0.1 g Total Fat (0 g Mono, 0 g Poly, 0 g Sat); 0 mg Cholesterol; 17 g Carbohydrate; trace Fibre; 0 g Protein; 16 mg Sodium

Variation (without alcohol): Omit cherry brandy. Reserve syrup from canned cherries. Add 1/2 cup (125 mL) reserved syrup to punch.

Sparkling Strawberry Bubbly

Sweet and fruity coral-coloured drink that's light and refreshing.

Sliced fresh strawberries	3 cups	750 mL
Icing (confectioner's) sugar	3/4 cup	175 mL
Orange-flavoured liqueur (such as Grand Marnier), 2 1/2 oz.	1/3 cup	75 mL
Bottles of sparkling dry white (or alcohol-free) wine (26 oz., 750 mL, each)	2	2
Sliced fresh strawberries (optional)	1 1/2 cups	375 mL

Process first 3 ingredients in blender until smooth. Transfer to small punch bowl.

Add wine and second amount of strawberries. Stir gently. Makes about 10 cups (2.5 L). Serves 18.

1 serving: 95 Calories; 0.1 g Total Fat (0 g Mono, 0.1 g Poly, 0 g Sat); 0 mg Cholesterol; 8 g Carbohydrate; 1 g Fibre; 0 g Protein; 5 mg Sodium

Serving Suggestion: This pretty punch looks best served in champagne flutes (see page 8).

Cold And Winey

Have this ready for the group after a day of outdoor winter activities.
The strong flavours will warm them from the inside out.

Orange juice	2 cups	500 mL
Lemon juice	1/2 cup	125 mL
Grenadine syrup	1/4 cup	60 mL
Frozen whole blackberries (or raspberries)	24	24
Bottles of dry red (or alcohol-free) wine (26 oz., 750 mL, each)	2	2
Blackberry brandy (4 oz.)	1/2 cup	125 mL
Orange-flavoured liqueur (such as Grand Marnier), 4 oz.	1/2 cup	125 mL
Granulated sugar	1/4 cup	60 mL

Combine orange juice, lemon juice and grenadine in 4 cup (1 L) liquid measure. Pour into ice cube trays for a total of 24 cubes. Add 1 blackberry to each cube. Freeze for at least 4 hours until firm.

Measure remaining 4 ingredients into small punch bowl. Stir until sugar is dissolved. Add frozen orange juice cubes. Makes about 8 1/2 cups (2.1 L). Serves 14.

1 serving: 176 Calories; 0.1 g Total Fat (0 g Mono, 0 g Poly, 0 g Sat); 0 mg Cholesterol;
17 g Carbohydrate; 1 g Fibre; 1 g Protein; 10 mg Sodium

Serving Suggestion: Serve in small wine glasses (see page 8) so your guests can appreciate its deep, rich colour.

Minted Citrus Punch

Sweet and refreshing citrus tang with a hint of mint.

Can of mandarin orange segments (with juice)	10 oz.	284 mL
Boiling water	4 cups	1 L
Fresh mint leaves	1 cup	250 mL
Peel of medium orange, white pith removed, cut into strips	1	1
Peel of medium lemon, white pith removed, cut into strips	1	1
Can of frozen concentrated lemonade, partially thawed	12 1/2 oz.	355 mL
Can of frozen concentrated orange juice, partially thawed	12 1/2 oz.	355 mL
Grapefruit soft drink	4 cups	1 L

Spoon mandarin orange segments and juice into ice cube tray for a total of about 12 cubes (see Note). Freeze for at least 4 hours until firm.

Pour boiling water into large heatproof bowl. Add mint and both peels. Stir. Cover. Let stand for 1 hour.

Strain mint mixture through sieve into small punch bowl. Discard solids. Add remaining 3 ingredients. Stir gently. Add frozen mandarin orange cubes. Makes about 10 1/2 cups (2.6 L). Serves 18.

1 serving: 111 Calories; 0.1 g Total Fat (0 g Mono, 0 g Poly, 0 g Sat); 0 mg Cholesterol; 28 g Carbohydrate; trace Fibre; 1 g Protein; 9 mg Sodium

Pictured on page 125.

Note: Add fresh mint leaves to mandarin orange segments in ice cube tray before freezing for extra colour and flavour.

Party Eggnog

Spicy, foamy eggnog your guests will love.

Large eggs (see Note)	12	12
Icing (confectioner's) sugar	2 cups	500 mL
Vanilla	3 tbsp.	50 mL
Salt	1/2 tsp.	2 mL
Homogenized milk	8 cups	2 L
Spiced rum (or brandy), 4 – 8 oz.	1/2 – 1 cup	125 – 250 mL
Ground nutmeg	1 tsp.	5 mL
Ground cinnamon	1/2 tsp.	2 mL

Beat eggs in large bowl until frothy.

Add icing sugar, 1/4 cup (60 mL) at a time while beating, until combined. Add vanilla and salt. Stir. Pour into small punch bowl.

Add remaining 4 ingredients. Stir well. Makes about 14 cups (3.5 L). Serve immediately. Serves 25.

1 serving: 142 Calories; 5.2 g Total Fat (1.7 g Mono, 0.4 g Poly, 2.5 g Sat); 115 mg Cholesterol; 15 g Carbohydrate; 0 g Fibre; 6 g Protein; 118 mg Sodium

Note: Eggs used in beverages should be cold. Remove eggs from refrigerator just before adding. Beverages containing uncooked egg should be served immediately.

Paré Pointer

Say cheers in Romanian: "Noroc!" (nor-OOK)

Ginger Lemonade

Pleasantly sweet and refreshing lemon ginger flavour.

Boiling water	3 cups	750 mL
Granulated sugar	1 1/2 cups	375 mL
Chopped, peeled gingerroot	1 cup	250 mL
Water	3 cups	750 mL
Lemon juice	1/2 cup	125 mL
Whole cloves	8	8
Ice		

Pour boiling water into large heatproof bowl. Add sugar and ginger. Stir until sugar is dissolved. Cover. Let stand for 2 hours. Strain through cheesecloth into separate large bowl. Squeeze cheesecloth to extract liquid. Discard ginger. Pour liquid into pitcher.

Add water, lemon juice and cloves. Stir. Cover. Chill for at least 4 hours until cold. Remove and discard cloves. Makes about 7 cups (1.75 L). Pour over ice in 8 chilled medium glasses. Serves 8.

1 serving: 157 Calories; 0 g Total Fat (0 g Mono, 0 g Poly, 0 g Sat); 0 mg Cholesterol; 41 g Carbohydrate; trace Fibre; 0 g Protein; 1 mg Sodium

Pineapple Delight

A thirst-quenching punch. The pineapple ice mold gives it extra flavour.

Pineapple juice	2 cups	500 mL
Ginger ale	8 cups	2 L
Pineapple juice	2 cups	500 mL
Can of pineapple tidbits (with juice)	14 oz.	398 mL
Apricot brandy (6 oz.)	3/4 cup	175 mL

Pour first amount of pineapple juice into 2 cup (500 mL) shallow jelly mold. Freeze for at least 4 hours until firm.

Measure remaining 4 ingredients into small punch bowl. Stir gently. Add frozen pineapple juice mold. Makes about 10 cups (2.5 L). Serves 22.

1 serving: 89 Calories; 0.1 g Total Fat (0 g Mono, 0 g Poly, 0 g Sat); 0 mg Cholesterol; 18 g Carbohydrate; trace Fibre; 0 g Protein; 7 mg Sodium

Orange Mango Punch

A thick, tropical-flavoured punch. You may need
a whisk to mix in the coconut milk.

Granulated sugar	1/4 cup	60 mL
Water	3 tbsp.	50 mL
Cans of sliced mango (with syrup), 14 oz. (398 mL) each	2	2
Orange juice	3 cups	750 mL
Can of coconut milk	14 oz.	398 mL
Orange-flavoured liqueur (such as Grand Marnier), 2 1/2 oz.	1/3 cup	75 mL
Yellow-coloured, licorice-flavoured liqueur (such as Galliano), 1 1/2 oz. (see Note)	3 tbsp.	50 mL
Ice cubes	12	12

Combine sugar and water in small saucepan. Bring to a boil on medium-high. Boil, uncovered, for about 1 minute until slightly thickened and sugar is dissolved. Remove from heat. Cool.

Chop portion of mango into 1/4 inch (6 mm) pieces to fill 1 cup (250 mL) measure. Set aside. Process remaining mango with syrup in blender until smooth.

Measure next 4 ingredients into small punch bowl. Add processed mango, chopped mango and sugar mixture. Stir. Add ice cubes. Makes about 9 cups (2.25 L). Serves 16.

1 serving: 127 Calories; 5.3 g Total Fat (0.3 g Mono, 0.1 g Poly, 4.5 g Sat); 0 mg Cholesterol; 16 g Carbohydrate; 1 g Fibre; 1 g Protein; 5 mg Sodium

Note: If you cannot find Galliano, add several drops of yellow food colouring to same amount of clear licorice-flavoured liqueur (such as Sambuca) until desired shade is reached.

Variation (without alcohol): Omit liqueurs. Use same amount of orange juice.

Serving Suggestion: Use mandarin-mint ice cubes (Minted Citrus Punch, page 119) for a special touch. If you prefer a less thick punch, add lemon lime soft drink or club soda until desired consistency.

Mocha Punch

*Chocolate syrup in the bottom of the glass gives
this creamy treat a layered look. Whipped cream and
grated chocolate add a special touch your guests will love.*

Hot strong prepared coffee (see Note)	4 cups	1 L
Granulated sugar	1/2 cup	125 mL
Salt	1/4 tsp.	1 mL
Cold strong prepared coffee (see Note)	4 cups	1 L
Chocolate ice cream	4 cups	1 L
Vanilla ice cream	4 cups	1 L
Almond flavouring	1/4 tsp.	1 mL
Chocolate syrup	3/4 cup	175 mL
Ice cubes	36	36

Whipped cream, for garnish
Grated chocolate, for garnish

Measure hot coffee, sugar and salt into large bowl. Stir until sugar is dissolved.

Add next 4 ingredients. Stir until ice cream is melted. Makes about 11 cups (2.75 L). Transfer to large pitcher.

Measure about 1 tbsp. (15 mL) chocolate syrup into each of 12 medium glasses. Add 3 ice cubes to each. Fill with ice cream mixture.

Garnish with whipped cream and grated chocolate. Serves 12.

1 serving: 278 Calories; 10.4 g Total Fat (3 g Mono, 0.4 g Poly, 6.4 g Sat); 36 mg Cholesterol; 46 g Carbohydrate; 0 g Fibre; 4 g Protein; 148 mg Sodium

Note: For extra-strong flavour, use espresso.

Serving Suggestion: Place small pitcher of chocolate syrup and a bucket of ice on buffet table. Write directions for making 1 glass of punch on pretty recipe card and set it beside pitcher of punch. Guests will have fun mixing their own drink! Be sure to have plenty of whipped cream and grated chocolate available.

Melon Lemonade

A delightful combination of fresh flavours.

Can of frozen concentrated lemonade, partially thawed	12 1/2 oz.	355 mL
White (light) rum (6 oz.)	3/4 cup	175 mL
Melon-flavoured liqueur (such as Bols), 4 oz.	1/2 cup	125 mL
Lemon lime soft drink	5 cups	1.25 L

Ice
Small honeydew slices, for garnish

Combine concentrated lemonade, rum and liqueur in pitcher. Add lemon lime soft drink. Stir gently. Makes about 8 cups (2 L).

Pour over ice in 8 large glasses. Garnish each with honeydew slice. Serves 8.

1 serving: 249 Calories; 0.1 g Total Fat (0 g Mono, 0 g Poly, 0 g Sat); 0 mg Cholesterol; 43 g Carbohydrate; 0 g Fibre; 0 g Protein; 20 mg Sodium

Pictured on front cover.

Serving Suggestion: Add small slices of honeydew and watermelon to water in ice cube trays. Freeze until firm. Makes pretty ice cubes for this, or any other, fruity beverage.

1. Minted Citrus Punch, page 119
2. Sangria, page 112
3. Rhubarb Punch, page 115

Props Courtesy Of: Dansk Gifts
Sears Canada
The Bay

Winter Season's Brew

A delectable hot drink full of spice.

Cranberry cocktail	4 cups	1 L
Pineapple juice	4 cups	1 L
Granulated sugar	1/3 cup	75 mL
Whole cloves	1 tbsp.	15 mL
Whole allspice	2 tsp.	10 mL
Cinnamon sticks (4 inches, 10 cm, each), broken up	4	4
Salt	1/4 tsp.	1 mL

Measure cranberry cocktail and pineapple juice into percolator (see Note). Insert stem and basket.

Place remaining 5 ingredients in basket. Perk as usual. Makes about 8 cups (2 L). Pour into 6 large mugs. Serves 6.

1 serving: 245 Calories; 0.3 g Total Fat (0 g Mono, 0.1 g Poly, 0.1 g Sat); 0 mg Cholesterol; 62 g Carbohydrate; trace Fibre; 1 g Protein; 104 mg Sodium

Note: Don't have a percolator? Measure cocktail and juice, sugar and salt into large saucepan. Stir. Tie spices in cheesecloth. Add to saucepan. Bring to a boil on medium. Reduce heat to medium-low. Simmer, uncovered, for about 20 minutes, stirring occasionally, until fragrant. Remove and discard cheesecloth with spices.

1. Peppercorn Vodka, page 149
2. Ginger Orange Liqueur, page 138
3. Hot Tequila Cider, page 132

Props Courtesy Of: Pier 1 Imports

Percolator Punch

This mellow, spiced fruit drink is perfect
for a relaxing evening shared with friends.

Apple cider (or juice)	4 cups	1 L
Orange juice	4 cups	1 L
Cranberry cocktail	4 cups	1 L
Lemon juice	2 tbsp.	30 mL
Salt	1/8 tsp.	0.5 mL
Brown sugar, packed	3/4 cup	175 mL
Cinnamon stick (4 inches, 10 cm), broken up	1	1
Whole cloves	1 1/2 tsp.	7 mL
Whole allspice	1 1/2 tsp.	7 mL

Measure first 5 ingredients into percolator (see Note). Insert stem and basket.

Place remaining 4 ingredients in basket. Perk as usual. Makes about 12 cups (3 L). Pour into 12 small mugs. Serves 12.

1 serving: 187 Calories; 0.4 g Total Fat (0 g Mono, 0.1 g Poly, 0.1 g Sat); 0 mg Cholesterol; 47 g Carbohydrate; trace Fibre; 1 g Protein; 37 mg Sodium

Note: Don't have a percolator? Measure first 5 ingredients and brown sugar into large saucepan. Stir. Tie spices in cheesecloth. Add to saucepan. Bring to a boil on medium. Reduce heat to medium-low. Simmer, uncovered, for about 20 minutes, stirring occasionally, until fragrant. Remove and discard cheesecloth with spices.

Paré Pointer

Say cheers in Russian: "Na Zdrovia!" (NAH zdor-OH-vEEa)

Warm Spiced Rum

Clear, golden colour with lightly spiced apple flavour. Soothing and warming.

Apple cider	6 cups	1.5 L
Apple juice	1 cup	250 mL
Whole allspice	8	8
Cinnamon sticks (4 inches, 10 cm, each)	2	2
Spiced rum (4 oz.)	1/2 cup	125 mL
Brandy (1 1/2 oz.)	3 tbsp.	50 mL

Measure first 4 ingredients into large saucepan. Stir. Heat on medium for 20 to 30 minutes, stirring occasionally, until fragrant.

Add rum and brandy. Stir. Remove from heat. Strain through sieve into heatproof pitcher. Discard solids. Makes about 7 cups (1.75 L). Pour into 8 small mugs. Serves 8.

1 serving: 154 Calories; 0.3 g Total Fat (0 g Mono, 0.1 g Poly, 0 g Sat); 0 mg Cholesterol; 27 g Carbohydrate; trace Fibre; 0 g Protein; 7 mg Sodium

Warm Apricot Honey Punch

A sweet, delicious way to warm up after skiing or skating.

Apricot nectar	6 cups	1.5 L
Liquid honey	3 tbsp.	50 mL
Lemon juice	2 tbsp.	30 mL
Medium orange, sliced thinly	1	1

Heat and stir apricot nectar, honey and lemon juice in large saucepan on medium until just boiling. Remove from heat. Makes about 6 cups (1.5 L).

Pour into 6 large mugs. Garnish each with orange slice. Serves 6.

1 serving: 192 Calories; 0.3 g Total Fat (0.1 g Mono, 0.1 g Poly, 0 g Sat); 0 mg Cholesterol; 50 g Carbohydrate; 2 g Fibre; 1 g Protein; 8 mg Sodium

Golden Wedding Punch

Pleasantly sweet citrus and apple combination bubbling with flavour.

Apple juice	4 cups	1 L
Can of frozen concentrated lemonade, partially thawed	12 1/2 oz.	355 mL
Can of frozen concentrated orange juice, partially thawed	12 1/2 oz.	355 mL
Ginger ale	8 cups	2 L

Combine first 3 ingredients in small punch bowl. Add ginger ale. Stir gently. Makes about 15 1/2 cups (3.75 L). Serves 28.

1 serving: 95 Calories; 0.1 g Total Fat (0 g Mono, 0 g Poly, 0 g Sat); 0 mg Cholesterol; 24 g Carbohydrate; trace Fibre; 0 g Protein; 7 mg Sodium

Variation (with alcohol): Add 1 1/2 cups (375 mL, 13 oz.) gin (or vodka) to punch.

Serving Suggestion: Make Ice Ring, page 114, using orange and lemon slices. Add to punch in large punch bowl. Arrange small glasses around punch bowl for an attractive presentation.

Cranberry Lime Sparkle

A refreshing balance of tart and sweet in a drink.
Cranberry Lime Punch (below) is a simple yet elegant way
to dress up your holiday party, with or without alcohol.

Cranberry cocktail	1/3 cup	75 mL
Lime cordial (alcohol-free)	1 tbsp.	15 mL
Sparkling dry white (or alcohol-free) wine	2/3 cup	150 mL

Measure cranberry cocktail and lime cordial into small glass.

Top with sparkling wine. Stir gently. Makes about 1 cup (250 mL).
Serves 1.

1 serving: 168 Calories; 0 g Total Fat (0 g Mono, 0 g Poly, 0 g Sat); 0 mg Cholesterol; 16 g Carbohydrate; trace Fibre; 0 g Protein; 10 mg Sodium

CRANBERRY GINGER SPARKLE: Omit sparkling wine. Use same amount of ginger ale.

CRANBERRY LEMON SPARKLE: Omit sparkling wine. Use same amount of lemon lime soft drink.

CRANBERRY LIME PUNCH: Measure 1/2 cup (125 mL) lime cordial, 3 cups (750 mL) cranberry cocktail and 6 cups (1.5 L) sparkling dry white (or alcohol-free) wine into small punch bowl. Stir gently. Makes about 9 1/2 cups (2.4 L). Serves 10.

Paré Pointer
Say cheers in Gaelic: "Schlante!" (sh-LAHN-tee)

Cranberry Champagne

Something a little different, but a lovely combination of flavours.

Bottles of sparkling dry white (or alcohol-free) wine (26 oz., 750 mL, each)	2	2
Cranberry cocktail	1 1/2 cups	375 mL
Orange-flavoured liqueur (such as Grand Marnier), 2 oz.	1/4 cup	60 mL

Measure all 3 ingredients into small punch bowl or large pitcher. Stir gently. Makes about 8 1/2 cups (2.1 L). Serves 12.

1 serving: 115 Calories; 0 g Total Fat (0 g Mono, 0 g Poly, 0 g Sat); 0 mg Cholesterol; 6 g Carbohydrate; 0 g Fibre; 0 g Protein; 7 mg Sodium

Pictured on front cover.

Serving Suggestion: Show off this pretty mixture by serving it in champagne flutes (see page 8).

Hot Tequila Cider

Seamless blend of tequila, apple and cinnamon in a pale red cider.

Sparkling apple cider (with alcohol)	4 cups	1 L
Cranberry cocktail	1 1/2 cups	375 mL
Tequila (2 oz.)	1/4 cup	60 mL
Orange-flavoured liqueur (such as Grand Marnier), 2 oz.	1/4 cup	60 mL
Cinnamon sticks (4 inches, 10 cm, each)	2	2

Heat and stir all 5 ingredients in large saucepan on medium-low for about 20 minutes until hot. Do not boil. Remove and discard cinnamon sticks. Makes about 6 cups (1.5 L). Pour into 6 small mugs. Serves 6.

1 serving: 166 Calories; 0.1 g Total Fat (0 g Mono, 0 g Poly, 0 g Sat); 0 mg Cholesterol; 20 g Carbohydrate; 0 g Fibre; 0 g Protein; 16 mg Sodium

Pictured on page 126.

Strawberry Cupid

A pretty pink drink for Valentine's Day with a creamy strawberry taste.
Adults will love it as much as the kids will!

Boiling water	1/2 cup	125 mL
Package of strawberry-flavoured jelly powder (gelatin)	3 oz.	85 g
Strawberry ice cream	2 cups	500 mL
Milk	1 cup	250 mL
Crushed ice	1/2 cup	125 mL

Pour boiling water into 2 cup (500 mL) liquid measure. Add jelly powder. Stir until dissolved. Let stand for 5 minutes. Transfer to blender. Process on medium for 1 minute.

Add ice cream, 1/4 cup (60 mL) at a time (about 1 scoop), processing after each addition until smooth.

Add milk and crushed ice. Process for 30 seconds. Makes about 4 cups (1 L). Pour into 4 chilled medium glasses. Serves 4.

1 serving: 242 Calories; 6.5 g Total Fat (0.2 g Mono, 0 g Poly, 0.4 g Sat); 23 mg Cholesterol; 42 g Carbohydrate; 0 g Fibre; 6 g Protein; 128 mg Sodium

Pictured on page 144.

Variation: Try other flavours of jelly powder with vanilla ice cream for a new taste experience.

Paré Pointer
Say cheers in Spanish: "Salud!" (SAH-lood)

Malted Easter Egg

Creamy chocolate with subtle malt flavour.
Kids will love the marshmallow flavour and crunchy sprinkles.

Chocolate ice cream	2 cups	500 mL
Milk	1 cup	250 mL
Miniature marshmallows	1/4 cup	60 mL
Malt drink mix (such as Ovaltine)	2 tbsp.	30 mL
Coloured candy sprinkles, for garnish	1 tbsp.	15 mL

Process first 4 ingredients in blender for about 1 minute until frothy. Makes about 2 3/4 cups (675 mL). Pour into 2 chilled medium glasses.

Garnish each with candy sprinkles. Serves 2.

1 serving: 412 Calories; 17.1 g Total Fat (5 g Mono, 0.7 g Poly, 10.5 g Sat); 53 mg Cholesterol; 59 g Carbohydrate; 0 g Fibre; 10 g Protein; 236 mg Sodium

Pictured on page 144.

Paré Pointer
Say cheers in Swedish: "Skal!" (SKOHL)

Witch's Brew

A deep red, cherry-flavoured beverage—just right for your Halloween party.

Cranberry-apple juice	4 cups	1 L
Orange juice	1 cup	250 mL
Maraschino cherry juice	1/4 cup	60 mL
Cinnamon stick (4 inches, 10 cm)	1	1
Whole cloves	3	3
Whole allspice	3	3
Medium orange, sliced thinly (optional)	1	1
Maraschino cherries (optional)	4	4

Measure first 6 ingredients into large saucepan. Bring to a boil on medium-high. Reduce heat to medium-low. Simmer, uncovered, for 15 minutes, stirring occasionally. Remove from heat. Strain through sieve into 4 cup (1 L) liquid measure. Discard solids. Makes about 4 cups (1 L).

Place 1 or 2 orange slices and 1 maraschino cherry in each of 4 small mugs. Pour cranberry mixture over top of each. Serves 4.

1 serving: 208 Calories; 0.1 g Total Fat (0 g Mono, 0 g Poly, 0 g Sat); 0 mg Cholesterol; 52 g Carbohydrate; trace Fibre; 1 g Protein; 6 mg Sodium

Pictured on page 143.

Serving Suggestion: Cool this brew slightly when serving to children. To make a special brew for adults, omit maraschino cherry juice. Add 1/4 cup (60 mL) cherry brandy to strained, hot cranberry mixture. Stir. Pour into small mugs. Garnish with orange slices.

Nuclear Waste

Bright neon green with a slightly cloudy appearance. Looks radioactive!
Alcohol taste is masked by citrus flavours, so be warned!

Orange juice	4 cups	1 L
Blue-coloured, orange-flavoured liqueur (such as Blue Curaçao), 4 oz. (see Note)	1/2 cup	125 mL
Vodka (2 1/2 oz.)	1/3 cup	75 mL
Ginger ale	3 cups	750 mL
Ice		

Combine orange juice, liqueur and vodka in small punch bowl or large pitcher. Chill for about 3 hours until cold.

Just before serving, add ginger ale. Stir gently. Makes about 8 cups (2 L). Pour over ice in 8 medium glasses. Serves 8.

1 serving: 176 Calories; 0.3 g Total Fat (0.1 g Mono, 0.1 g Poly, 0.1 g Sat); 0 mg Cholesterol; 31 g Carbohydrate; trace Fibre; 1 g Protein; 10 mg Sodium

Pictured on page 143.

Note: If you cannot find Blue Curaçao, add several drops of blue liquid food colouring to same amount of clear Curaçao until desired shade is reached.

Swamp Water

Visually fascinating—purple and orange jelly pieces suspended in a fizzy drink. Great for Halloween or a child's birthday party.

Package of grape-flavoured jelly powder (gelatin)	3 oz.	85 g
Package of orange-flavoured jelly powder (gelatin)	3 oz.	85 g
Prepared grape-flavoured drink	4 cups	1 L
Lemon lime soft drink	4 cups	1 L

Prepare jelly powders in two 8 x 8 inch (20 x 20 cm) pans, according to package directions. Chill for about 4 hours until firm. Flake with fork or cut into small shapes using cookie cutter. Transfer to small punch bowl.

Add grape drink and lemon lime soft drink. Stir gently. Makes about 12 3/4 cups (3.2 L). Serves 16.

1 serving: 96 Calories; 0 g Total Fat (0 g Mono, 0 g Poly, 0 g Sat); 0 mg Cholesterol; 24 g Carbohydrate; 0 g Fibre; 1 g Protein; 38 mg Sodium

Pictured on page 143.

Variation: Experiment with colours and flavours by changing jelly powders and prepared drink.

Paré Pointer
Say cheers in Thai: "Sawasdi!" (SAH-wahs-DEE)

Ginger Orange Liqueur

A little patience brings great reward—a mildly spiced, orange-flavoured liqueur.
Straining mixture through cheesecloth will result in a bright, clear appearance.

Vodka (26 oz.)	3 cups	750 mL
Grated orange zest	1/2 cup	125 mL
Piece of peeled gingerroot (3 inches, 7.5 cm), sliced	1	1
Granulated sugar	2/3 cup	150 mL
Water	1/3 cup	75 mL

Combine vodka, orange zest and ginger in sterile glass jar with tight-fitting lid. Let stand for 1 week at room temperature. Strain through sieve into 4 cup (1 L) liquid measure. Discard solids. Return liquid to same jar.

Combine sugar and water in small saucepan. Bring to a boil on medium. Heat and stir until sugar is dissolved. Remove from heat. Cool. Add to vodka mixture in jar. Makes about 3 1/2 cups (875 mL). Let stand for 1 week at room temperature. Strain through cheesecloth into 4 cup (1 L) liquid measure. Discard solids. Transfer to storage jar or fancy bottle with tight-fitting lid. Store for up to 1 month at room temperature or in refrigerator. Serves 30.

1 serving: 73 Calories; 0 g Total Fat (0 g Mono, 0 g Poly, 0 g Sat); 0 mg Cholesterol; 5 g Carbohydrate; 0 g Fibre; 0 g Protein; 0 mg Sodium

Pictured on page 126.

Serving Suggestion: Equally good served at room temperature or over ice. Use as substitute for orange-flavoured liqueurs in mixed drinks.

Orange Dream Liqueur

Creamy, thick orange liqueur—reminiscent of an orange ice cream bar.
Flavours will mellow with time. Makes a nice gift.

Water	1 cup	250 mL
Granulated sugar	1/2 cup	125 mL
Vodka (13 oz.)	1 1/2 cups	375 mL
Can of sweetened condensed milk	11 oz.	300 mL
Frozen concentrated orange juice	1/3 cup	75 mL
Vanilla	2 tsp.	10 mL

Measure water and sugar into small saucepan. Bring to a boil on medium. Heat and stir until sugar is dissolved. Remove from heat. Let stand until cooled completely.

Measure next 4 ingredients into blender. Add sugar mixture. Process for about 1 minute until smooth. Makes about 4 cups (1 L). Pour into sterile glass jar with tight-fitting lid. Store for up to 1 month in refrigerator. Serves 32.

1 serving: 83 Calories; 1.1 g Total Fat (0.3 g Mono, 0 g Poly, 0.7 g Sat); 4 mg Cholesterol; 11 g Carbohydrate; 0 g Fibre; 1 g Protein; 16 mg Sodium

Serving Suggestion: Serve over ice or in your favourite coffee.

ORANGE DREAM CLOUD: Pour equal amounts of Orange Dream Liqueur and club soda over ice in medium glass. Stir gently. Serves 1.

Paré Pointer
Say cheers in Turkish: "Serefe!" (sher-FAY)

Christmas Spirit

A robust, spiced berry liqueur to serve as an aperitif or after-dinner drink.
Can be used as a base for your Christmas punch, too.

Granulated sugar	2 cups	500 mL
Fresh (or frozen, thawed) raspberries	1 1/2 cups	375 mL
Fresh (or frozen, thawed) cranberries	1 1/3 cups	325 mL
Water	1 cup	250 mL
Medium orange, zest and juice only	1	1
Whole cloves	6	6
Whole allspice	4	4
Cinnamon sticks (4 inches, 10 cm, each)	2	2
Gin (or vodka), 26 oz.	3 cups	750 mL

Combine first 8 ingredients in large pot or Dutch oven. Bring to a boil on medium. Reduce heat to medium-low. Simmer, uncovered, for about 20 minutes until fragrant. Remove from heat. Cool.

Add gin. Stir well. Pour into 2 sterile 4 cup (1 L) glass jars with tight-fitting lids. Let stand at room temperature for 2 weeks. Shake gently once every 2 days. Strain through sieve into 8 cup (2 L) liquid measure. Do not push through. Gently lift berry mixture in sieve, using spoon, allowing liquid to flow through. Discard solids. Return liquid to same jars with tight-fitting lids. Let stand at room temperature for 2 weeks. Strain through double layer of cheesecloth into 2 cup (500 mL) liquid measure. Discard solids. Makes about 2 cups (500 mL). Transfer to storage jar or fancy bottle with tight-fitting lid. Store for up to 1 month at room temperature or in refrigerator. Serves 16.

1 serving: 211 Calories; 0.1 g Total Fat (0 g Mono, 0 g Poly, 0 g Sat); 0 mg Cholesterol;
28 g Carbohydrate; trace Fibre; 0 g Protein; 1 mg Sodium

Pictured on front cover.

Licorice Twist Nog

Here are just a few ways to add a twist to your favourite eggnog.
A nice change from the ordinary.

Ice cubes	3	3
Eggnog	3/4 cup	175 mL
Licorice-flavoured liqueur (such as Sambuca), 1/2 – 1 oz.	1 – 2 tbsp.	15 – 30 mL

Put ice cubes into medium glass. Add eggnog and liqueur. Stir. Makes about 1 cup (250 mL). Serves 1.

1 serving: 335 Calories; 15.2 g Total Fat (4.5 g Mono, 0.7 g Poly, 9 g Sat); 118 mg Cholesterol; 34 g Carbohydrate; 0 g Fibre; 8 g Protein; 111 mg Sodium

TROPICAL TWIST NOG: Measure 1 tbsp. (15 mL, 1/2 oz.) each, banana-flavoured liqueur (such as Crème de banane) and coconut-flavoured rum (such as Malibu), over ice in medium glass. Add 1 cup (250 mL) eggnog. Stir. Sprinkle with toasted coconut (see Tip, page 23). Serves 1.

ORANGE TWIST NOG: Measure 1 tbsp. (15 mL, 1/2 oz.) Orange Dream Liqueur, page 139, 1 tbsp. (15 mL) frozen concentrated orange juice and 2/3 cup (150 mL) eggnog into cocktail shaker. Add ice cubes. Replace lid. Hold firmly and shake vigorously until cold. Strain through sieve into small glass. Sprinkle with ground ginger. Serves 1.

Pictured on page 144.

Paré Pointer

Say cheers in Yugoslavian: "Zivio!" (ziv-EE-oh)

Hot Buttered Cranberry

Rich, buttery cranberry and spice. Tastes great!

Cans of jellied cranberry sauce (14 oz., 398 mL, each)	2	2
Pineapple juice	4 cups	1 L
Water	3 cups	750 mL
Brown sugar, packed	1/2 cup	125 mL
Ground cinnamon	1/2 tsp.	2 mL
Ground cloves	1/2 tsp.	2 mL
Ground nutmeg	1/4 tsp.	1 mL
Ground allspice	1/4 tsp.	1 mL
Salt	1/8 tsp.	0.5 mL
Butter (not margarine)	1/4 cup	60 mL
Navy (dark) rum (8 oz.), optional	1 cup	250 mL

Measure first 9 ingredients into 3 1/2 quart (3 1/2 L) slow cooker. Stir well. Cover. Cook on Low for 4 hours.

Add butter and rum. Stir until butter is melted. Makes about 12 cups (3 L). Serves 12.

1 serving: 240 Calories; 4.3 g Total Fat (1.2 g Mono, 0.2 g Poly, 2.6 g Sat); 11 mg Cholesterol; 52 g Carbohydrate; 1 g Fibre; 0 g Protein; 95 mg Sodium

HOT SPICED CRANBERRY: Omit butter.

1. Nuclear Waste, page 136
2. Witch's Brew, page 135
3. Swamp Water, page 137

Props Courtesy Of: Casa Bugatti
Dansk Gifts

Melted Snowball

Sweet butterscotch and spiced rum will warm and relax you.
Great after a day of outdoor winter activities.

Butter (not margarine), softened	2/3 cup	150 mL
Brown sugar, packed	1 1/2 cups	375 mL
Icing (confectioner's) sugar	1 cup	250 mL
Vanilla ice cream, softened	2 cups	500 mL
Spiced rum (8 oz.)	1 cup	250 mL
Boiling water	6 cups	1.5 L

Beat butter in large bowl until smooth. Add brown sugar and icing sugar. Beat until thick and creamy.

Add ice cream. Stir until well combined. Makes about 4 cups (1 L) ice cream mixture. Transfer to plastic container with tight-fitting lid. Freeze for at least 6 hours until firm.

Scoop about 1/2 cup (125 mL) ice cream mixture (about 2 scoops) into each of 8 large mugs. Add 2 tbsp. (30 mL, 1 oz.) rum and 3/4 cup (175 mL) boiling water to each. Stir. Serves 8.

1 serving: 507 Calories; 20.1 g Total Fat (5.8 g Mono, 0.8 g Poly, 12.5 g Sat); 59 mg Cholesterol; 66 g Carbohydrate; 0 g Fibre; 1 g Protein; 211 mg Sodium

1. Malted Easter Egg, page 134
2. Orange Twist Nog, page 141
3. Strawberry Cupid, page 133

Props Courtesy Of: Dansk Gifts
Pier 1 Imports

Slow Cooker Wassail

Pronounced WAH-sul or WAH-sayl.
A warming winter beverage any way you say it!

Cinnamon sticks (4 inches, 10 cm, each)	2	2
Whole allspice	12	12
Peel of small orange, white pith removed, chopped	1	1
Piece of peeled gingerroot (about 1 inch, 2.5 cm), chopped	1	1
Apple cider	12 cups	3 L
Liquid honey (optional)	1/3 cup	75 mL

Place cinnamon sticks and allspice in small plastic bag. Pound with hammer or meat mallet until crushed. Transfer to 6 inch (15 cm) square double layer of cheesecloth.

Add orange peel and ginger. Tie cheesecloth with string to enclose spices.

Pour apple cider into 4 quart (4 L) slow cooker. Add honey. Stir. Add spice bag. Cook on Low for about 6 hours or on High for about 3 hours until fragrant. Remove and discard spice bag. Makes about 12 1/2 cups (3.1 L). Serves 12.

1 serving: 123 Calories; 0.3 g Total Fat (0 g Mono, 0.1 g Poly, 0.1 g Sat); 0 mg Cholesterol; 31 g Carbohydrate; trace Fibre; 0 g Protein; 8 mg Sodium

Variation (with alcohol): Add 1 cup (250 mL, 8 oz.) brandy or apple brandy near end of cooking time.

Paré Pointer
Say cheers in Norwegian: "Skal!" (SKAHL)

Spiced Peach Eggnog

Peach-flavoured eggnog with potent spiced rum. A little goes a long way.

Egg yolks (large), see Note	3	3
Icing (confectioner's) sugar	1/4 cup	60 mL
Sweetened powdered peach-flavoured drink crystals	1/4 cup	60 mL
Spiced rum (4 – 8 oz.)	1/2 – 1 cup	125 – 250 mL
Half-and-half cream (or milk)	2 cups	500 mL
Peach schnapps (2 oz.)	1/4 cup	60 mL
Egg whites (large), see Note	3	3
Ground nutmeg, sprinkle		

Beat egg yolks in medium bowl for about 5 minutes until pale.

Slowly add icing sugar and drink crystals while beating until well combined.

Slowly add rum while beating until drink crystals are dissolved. Cover. Chill for at least 1 hour until cold.

Add half-and-half cream and peach schnapps. Stir.

Beat egg whites in separate medium bowl with clean beaters until soft peaks form. Fold rum mixture into egg whites until no white streaks remain. Makes about 5 1/2 cups (1.4 L). Pour into 10 chilled small glasses.

Sprinkle each with nutmeg. Serves 10.

1 serving: 155 Calories; 6.6 g Total Fat (2.1 g Mono, 0.4 g Poly, 3.7 g Sat); 81 mg Cholesterol; 11 g Carbohydrate; 0 g Fibre; 3 g Protein; 46 mg Sodium

Note: Eggs used in beverages should be cold. Remove eggs from refrigerator just before adding. Beverages containing uncooked egg should be served immediately.

Brandy Mint Cream

Make ahead and refrigerate—stays thick for at least one hour.
Great as an after-dinner drink or dessert.

Vanilla ice cream, softened	4 cups	1 L
Brandy (4 oz.)	1/2 cup	125 mL
Mint-flavoured liqueur (such as Crème de menthe), 2 oz.	1/4 cup	60 mL

Process all 3 ingredients in blender until smooth. Makes about 5 cups (1.25 L). Pour into 6 chilled small glasses. Serves 6.

1 serving: 276 Calories; 10.3 g Total Fat (3 g Mono, 0.4 g Poly, 6.3 g Sat); 41 mg Cholesterol; 27 g Carbohydrate; 0 g Fibre; 3 g Protein; 75 mg Sodium

Serving Suggestion: Use green Crème de menthe instead of clear for a festive Christmas treat. Serve in parfait glasses or champagne flutes (see page 8)—just add a straw and enjoy!

Mulled Wine

Rich, red wine colour and flavour with citrus and spice tones.
Use a full-bodied red wine for best results.

Water	2 cups	500 mL
Granulated sugar	1/2 cup	125 mL
Whole cloves	8	8
Cinnamon stick (4 inches, 10 cm)	1	1
Dry red (or alcohol-free) wine (26 oz.)	3 cups	750 mL
Medium orange, sliced thinly	1	1

Measure first 4 ingredients into large saucepan. Bring to a boil on medium. Reduce heat to medium-low. Simmer, uncovered, for 10 to 15 minutes, stirring occasionally, until sugar is dissolved and mixture is fragrant. Remove and discard cloves and cinnamon stick.

Add wine and orange slices. Heat and stir until just hot. Do not boil. Makes about 6 cups (1.5 L). Pour into 6 small mugs. Place 1 orange slice in each. Serves 6.

1 serving: 168 Calories; 0 g Total Fat (0 g Mono, 0 g Poly, 0 g Sat); 0 mg Cholesterol; 22 g Carbohydrate; trace Fibre; 0 g Protein; 6 mg Sodium

Peppercorn Vodka

Spicy and warming. Use instead of regular vodka when you want to kick things up a notch. Will keep for up to one year, tightly sealed. Makes a great spicy Caesar.

Vodka (13 oz.)	1 1/2 cups	375 mL
Whole black peppercorns	2 tbsp.	30 mL

Combine vodka and peppercorns in sterile glass jar with tight-fitting lid. Let stand at room temperature for 1 week. Shake gently once a day. Strain through sieve into storage jar or fancy bottle with tight-fitting lid. Discard solids. Makes about 1 1/2 cups (375 mL). Serves 12.

1 serving: 68 Calories; 0 g Total Fat (0 g Mono, 0 g Poly, 0 g Sat); 0 mg Cholesterol; 0 g Carbohydrate; 0 g Fibre; 0 g Protein; 0 mg Sodium

Pictured on page 126.

SPICY CAESAR: Dampen rim of cocktail glass with lime wedge, or dip into lime juice in saucer. Press into salt in separate saucer until coated. Pour 2 tbsp. (30 mL, 1 oz.) Peppercorn Vodka over ice in glass. Add clam tomato beverage to fill.

Paré Pointer
Say cheers in Latin: Propino Tibi Salutem!
(proh-PEEN-oh tib-EE sa-LOO-tem)

Measurement Tables

Spoons

Conventional Measure	Metric Exact Conversion Millilitre (mL)	Metric Standard Measure Millilitre (mL)
1/8 teaspoon (tsp.)	0.6 mL	0.5 mL
1/4 teaspoon (tsp.)	1.2 mL	1 mL
1/2 teaspoon (tsp.)	2.4 mL	2 mL
1 teaspoon (tsp.)	4.7 mL	5 mL
2 teaspoons (tsp.)	9.4 mL	10 mL
1 tablespoon (tbsp.)	14.2 mL	15 mL

Cups

Conventional Measure	Metric Exact Conversion Millilitre (mL)	Metric Standard Measure Millilitre (mL)
1/4 cup (4 tbsp.)	56.8 mL	60 mL
1/3 cup (5 1/3 tbsp.)	75.6 mL	75 mL
1/2 cup (8 tbsp.)	113.7 mL	125 mL
2/3 cup (10 2/3 tbsp.)	151.2 mL	150 mL
3/4 cup (12 tbsp.)	170.5 mL	175 mL
1 cup (16 tbsp.)	227.3 mL	250 mL
4 1/2 cups	1022.9 mL	1000 mL (1 L)

Oven Temperatures

Fahrenheit (°F)	Celsius (°C)
175°	80°
200°	95°
225°	110°
250°	120°
275°	140°
300°	150°
325°	160°
350°	175°
375°	190°
400°	205°
425°	220°
450°	230°
475°	240°
500°	260°

Dry Measurements

Conventional Measure Ounces (oz.)	Metric Exact Conversion Grams (g)	Metric Standard Measure Grams (g)
1 oz.	28.3 g	28 g
2 oz.	56.7 g	57 g
3 oz.	85.0 g	85 g
4 oz.	113.4 g	125 g
5 oz.	141.7 g	140 g
6 oz.	170.1 g	170 g
7 oz.	198.4 g	200 g
8 oz.	226.8 g	250 g
16 oz.	453.6 g	500 g
32 oz.	907.2 g	1000 g (1 kg)

Pans

Conventional Inches	Metric Centimetres
8x8 inch	20x20 cm
9x9 inch	22x22 cm
9x13 inch	22x33 cm
10x15 inch	25x38 cm
11x17 inch	28x43 cm
8x2 inch round	20x5 cm
9x2 inch round	22x5 cm
10x4 1/2 inch tube	25x11 cm
8x4x3 inch loaf	20x10x7.5 cm
9x5x3 inch loaf	22x12.5x7.5 cm

Casseroles

CANADA & BRITAIN Standard Size Casserole	Exact Metric Measure	UNITED STATES Standard Size Casserole	Exact Metric Measure
1 qt. (5 cups)	1.13 L	1 qt. (4 cups)	900 mL
1 1/2 qts. (7 1/2 cups)	1.69 L	1 1/2 qts. (6 cups)	1.35 L
2 qts. (10 cups)	2.25 L	2 qts. (8 cups)	1.8 L
2 1/2 qts. (12 1/2 cups)	2.81 L	2 1/2 qts. (10 cups)	2.25 L
3 qts. (15 cups)	3.38 L	3 qts. (12 cups)	2.7 L
4 qts. (20 cups)	4.5 L	4 qts. (16 cups)	3.6 L
5 qts. (25 cups)	5.63 L	5 qts. (20 cups)	4.5 L

Recipe Index

152

153

154

155

156

Company's Coming cookbooks are available at retail locations throughout Canada!

EXCLUSIVE mail order offer on next page

Buy any 2 cookbooks—choose a 3rd FREE of equal or lesser value than the lowest price paid.

Original Series — CA$15.99 Canada — US$12.99 USA & International

CODE		CODE		CODE	
SQ	150 Delicious Squares	SF	Stir-Fry	PK	The Pork Book
CA	Casseroles	MAM	Make-Ahead Meals	RL	Recipes For Leftovers
MU	Muffins & More	PB	The Potato Book	EB	The Egg Book
SA	Salads	CCLFC	Low-Fat Cooking	SDPP	School Days Party Pack
AP	Appetizers	CFK	Cook For Kids	HS	Herbs & Spices
SS	Soups & Sandwiches	SCH	Stews, Chilies & Chowders	BEV	The Beverage Book
CO	Cookies	FD	Fondues	SCD	Slow Cooker Dinners
PA	Pasta	CCBE	The Beef Book	WM	30-Minute Weekday Meals
BA	Barbecues	RC	The Rookie Cook	SDL	School Days Lunches
PR	Preserves	RHR	Rush-Hour Recipes	PD	Potluck Dishes
CH	Chicken, Etc.	SW	Sweet Cravings	GBR	Ground Beef Recipes
KC	Kids Cooking	YRG	Year-Round Grilling	FRIR	4-Ingredient Recipes
CT	Cooking For Two	GG	Garden Greens	KHC	Kids' Healthy Cooking
SC	Slow Cooker Recipes	CHC	Chinese Cooking		**NEW** July 1/06

3-in-1 Cookbook Collection

CODE	CA$29.99 Canada US$24.99 USA & International
QEE	Quick & Easy Entertaining
MNT	Meals in No Time **NEW** August 1/06

Lifestyle Series

CODE	CA$19.99 Canada US$15.99 USA & International
DC	Diabetic Cooking
DDI	Diabetic Dinners
LCR	Low-Carb Recipes
HR	Easy Healthy Recipes

Most Loved Recipe Collection

CODE	CA$23.99 Canada US$19.99 USA & International
MLA	Most Loved Appetizers
MLMC	Most Loved Main Courses
MLT	Most Loved Treats
MLBQ	Most Loved Barbecuing
MLCO	Most Loved Cookies

CODE	CA$24.99 Canada US$19.99 USA & International
MLSD	Most Loved Salads & Dressings

Special Occasion Series

CODE	CA$20.99 Canada US$19.99 USA & International
GFK	Gifts from the Kitchen

CODE	CA$24.99 Canada US$19.99 USA & International
BSS	Baking—Simple to Sensational
CGFK	Christmas Gifts from the Kitchen
TR	Timeless Recipes for All Occasions

Cookbook Author Biography

CODE	CA$15.99 Canada US$12.99 USA & International
JP	Jean Paré: An Appetite for Life

COOKBOOKS®

Company's Coming Publishing Limited
2311 – 96 Street
Edmonton, Alberta
Canada T6N 1G3
Tel: 780-450-6223
Fax: 780-450-1857
www.companyscoming.com

Order **ONLINE** for fast delivery!

Log onto **www.companyscoming.com**, browse through our library of cookbooks, gift sets and newest releases and place your order using our fast and secure online order form.

Title	Code	Quantity	Price	Total
			$	$
DON'T FORGET to indicate your FREE BOOK(S). (see exclusive mail order offer above) please print				

TOTAL BOOKS (including FREE)		TOTAL BOOKS PURCHASED:	$

	International	Canada & USA
Shipping & Handling First Book (per destination)	$ 11.98 (one book)	$ 5.98 (one book)
Additional Books (include FREE books)	$ ($4.99 each)	$ ($1.99 each)
Sub-Total	$	$
Canadian residents add G.S.T.(7%)		$
TOTAL AMOUNT ENCLOSED	$	$

Terms

- All orders must be prepaid. Sorry, no C.O.D.'s
- Prices are listed in Canadian Funds for Canadian orders, or US funds for US & International orders.
- Prices are subject to change without prior notice.
- Canadian residents must pay 7% G.S.T. (no provincial tax required)
- No tax is required for orders outside Canada.
- Satisfaction is guaranteed or return within 30 days for a full refund.
- Make cheque or money order payable to: **Company's Coming Publishing Limited.**
- Orders are shipped surface mail. For courier rates, visit our website: **www.companyscoming.com** or contact us: Tel: 780-450-6223 Fax: 780-450-1857.

Gift Giving

- Let us help you with your gift giving!
- We will send cookbooks directly to the recipients of your choice if you give us their names and addresses.
- Please specify the titles you wish to send to each person.
- If you would like to include your personal note or card, we will be pleased to enclose it with your gift order.
- Company's Coming Cookbooks make excellent gifts: birthdays, bridal showers, Mother's Day, Father's Day, graduation or any occasion ...collect them all!

☐ MasterCard ☐ VISA Expiry ___ / ___ MO/YR

Credit Card # _____

Name of cardholder _____

Cardholder signature _____

Shipping Address Send the cookbooks listed above to:

☐ Please check if this is a Gift Order

Name: _____

Street: _____

City: _____ Prov./State: _____

Postal Code/Zip: _____ Country: _____

Tel: (___) _____

E-mail address: _____

Your privacy is important to us. We will not share your e-mail address or personal information with any outside party.

☐ **YES! Please add me to your newsletter e-mail list.**

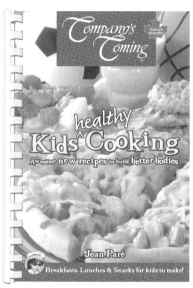

Hey kids! Want great muscles, goal-scoring energy, extra brainpower and shinier hair? *Kids' Healthy Cooking* shows you how to whip up the dishes that help make this happen. Try these healthier versions of your favourite recipes for faster, stronger, smarter bodies.

Company's Coming
COOKBOOKS®

Quick
&
Easy
Recipes

Everyday
Ingredients

Canada's
most popular
cookbooks!